A CENTURY OF POEMS

from the pages of the *TLS*,
1902–2002

Edited by Mick Imlah
and Alan Jenkins

First edition published in Great Britain in 2002 by
The Times Literary Supplement
Admiral House, 66-68 East Smithfield
London E1W 1BX

2 4 6 8 10 9 7 5 3 1

Copyright © 2002, The Times Literary Supplement

A CIP catalogue record for this book is available from the British Library

ISBN 1-84122-064-7

Printed and bound in England by the Bath Press Ltd

CONTENTS

Foreword

TLS – A CENTURY OF POEMS

Acknowledgements

FOREWORD

This is a selection of the best poems (or, in one or two cases, otherwise interesting poems) published in *The Times Literary Supplement* from its inception in January 1902 to the present centenary year. Each poet is represented by a single poem. None of the poems had previously appeared elsewhere, though some have since become well known.

In the early years of the paper, poems were generally included as an illustration of, or a commentary on, the triumphs and fears of Britain in the world, unless they were momentary pastoral or spiritual distractions from those. One weary piece from this period, by John Fethaland, asks "What liquid light or globes / Of fire celestial / Shall now my spirit dark illume or flame?" (It was entitled "Rejected": as well it might have been.) The avant garde was declined, if it was ever sent. After the onset of the First World War, poems in the *TLS* had the flavour of the Laureate about them – whoever wrote them. Some, like Thomas Hardy's "The Song of the Soldiers", with which this anthology begins, remain famous; others have gone with their makers into the dark.

The *TLS* published no poems between 1917 and 1936; as a result of this policy, John Masefield (whose poems appeared regularly in *The Times* instead) is the only one of seven Poet Laureates of the twentieth century – from Alfred Austin to the present incumbent, Andrew Motion – not to have contributed verse to the paper.

During the Second World War, the *TLS* published poems by Alun Lewis and Keith Douglas, both of whom subsequently died in the conflict. New verse was considered very much an adjunct to the main event: Edith Sitwell's "Still Falls the Rain", for example, when it was printed in 1941, was surrounded by a review of a book about the war in the air.

In the two decades following the war, the paper's attitude towards new poetry was erratic, but many fine poems were published. In 1954 and again in 1959, special issues featured pieces from the best of contemporary American poets. In the

1960s, the TLS exhibited a favouritism (while also publishing Adrian Henri and Roger McGough, before they became the "Liverpool School") towards poems translated – and sometimes not – from foreign languages: one weird choice was a translation into German of Edwin Muir's "An Franz Kafka", which we have been unable to include here.

Since 1970, however, the *TLS* has established itself as one of the most prestigious outlets for the very best of new poetry, whether written by the world-famous or the unknown; whether written originally in English, or translated from another tongue. Some of the finest long poems of recent decades, including Geoffrey Hill's "The Mystery of the Charity of Charles Péguy" and Paul Muldoon's "Incantata", have made their first appearance in our pages.

A Century of Poems also contains poems unpublished, for various reasons, by their authors in their lifetimes – Ivor Gurney, Rudyard Kipling and William Empson – but retrieved from obscurity by, respectively, Geoffrey Grigson, Thomas Pinney and John Haffenden, to whom our thanks are due, as they are to the literary estates of those concerned. We are indebted also to our predecessors on the staff with responsibility for choosing the poems, who at various times have included Edmund Blunden, G. S. Fraser, Ian Hamilton, Peter Porter, Blake Morrison and Alan Hollinghurst; to the poets or those representing them, for kindly allowing us to reprint; and finally to Jonathan Barnes and Tracy Luxford, whose powers of research and typing skills respectively made this publication possible.

MICK IMLAH
ALAN JENKINS

January 2002

THOMAS HARDY

Song of the Soldiers

What of the faith and fire within us
    Men who march away
    Ere the barn-cocks say
    Night is growing gray,
To hazards whence no tears can win us;
What of the faith and fire within us
Men who march away?

Is it a purblind prank, O think you,
    Friend with the musing eye
    Who watch us stepping by,
    With doubt and dolorous sigh?
Can much pondering so hoodwink you!
Is it a purblind prank, O think you,
    Friend with the musing eye?

Nay. We see well what we are doing
    Though some may not see –
    Dalliers as they be! –
    England's need are we;
Her distress would set us rueing:
Nay. We see well what we are doing,
    Though some may not see!

In our heart of hearts believing
    Victory crowns the just,
    And that braggarts must
    Surely bite the dust,
March we to the field ungrieving,
In our heart of hearts believing
    Victory crowns the just.

Hence the faith and fire within us
   Men who march away
   Ere the barn-cocks say
   Night is growing gray,
To hazards whence no tears can win us;
Hence the faith and fire within us
   Men who march away.

(September 10, 1914)

JOHN DRINKWATER

The Ships of Grief

On seas where every pilot fails
   A thousand thousand ships to-day
Ride with a moaning in their sails,
   Through winds grey and waters grey.

They are the ships of grief. They go
   As fleets are derelict and driven,
Estranged from every port they know,
   Scarce asking fortitude of heaven.

No, do not hail them. Let them ride
   Lonely as they would lonely be . . .
There is an hour will prove the tide,
   There is a sun will strike the sea.

(October 8, 1914)

ROBERT BRIDGES

Hell and Hate
(Description of a little picture)

Two demons thrust their arms out over the world,
    Hell with a ruddy torch of fire,
      And hate with gasping mouth,
    Striving to seize two children fair
Who play'd on the upper curve of the Earth.

Their shapes were vast as the thoughts of man,
      But the Earth was small
    As the moon's rim appeareth
    Scann'd through an optic glass.

The younger child stood erect on the Earth
    As a charioteer in a car
    Or a dancer with arm upraised;
    Her whole form – barely clad
    From feet to golden head –
Leapt brightly against the uttermost azure,
Whereon the stars were splashes of light
Dazed in the gulfing beds of space.

The elder might have been stell'd to show
The lady who led my boyish love;
But her face was graver than e'er to me
    When I look'd in her eyes long ago,
    And the hair on her shoulders fal'n
    Nested its luminous brown
    I' the downy spring of her wings:
Her figure aneath was screen'd by the Earth,
    Whereoff – so small that was
    No footing for her could be –
    She appeared to be sailing free
I' the glide and poise of her flight.

Then knew I the Angel Faith,
Who was guarding human Love.

Happy were both, of peaceful mien,
Contented as mankind longeth to be,
    Not merry as children are;
And show'd no fear of the Fiends' pursuit,
As ever those demons clutched in vain;
And I, who had fear'd awhile to see
Such gentleness in such jeopardy,
Lost fear myself; for I saw the foes
Were slipping aback and had no hold
On the round Earth that sped its course.

The painted figures never could move,
    But the artist's mind was there:
The long I look'd the more I knew
They were falling, falling away below
    To the darkness out of sight.

(These verses were written last year when, experimenting in prosody, I took this chance subject. I was dissatisfied with the attempt, and had laid them aside, till their existence recurred to my mind the other day. I now wish to publish them, thinking that the strange aptness of their meaning to the present unexpected situation may perhaps excuse their imperfection, and this somewhat lengthy explanation. The words have undergone no later adjustment.

R. B.)

(Written December 1913; published 1914)

LAURENCE BINYON

The Cause

Out of these throes that search and sear
   What is it so deep arises in us
Above the shaken thoughts of fear,
   Whatever thread the fates may spin us,
Above the horror that would drown
And tempest that would strike us down?

It is to stand in cleansing light,
   The cloud of dullard habit lifted,
To use a certainty of sight
   And breathe an air by peril sifted,
The things that once we deemed of price
Consumed in smoke of sacrifice.

It is to feel the world we knew
   Changed to a wonder past our knowing:
The grass, the trees, the skyey blue,
   The very stones are inly glowing
With something infinite, behind
These shadows, ardently divined.

We went our ways; each bosom bore
   Its spark of separate desire.
But now we kindle to the core
   With faith from this transfusing fire,
Thereto our inmost longings run
To be made infinitely one

With that which nothing can destroy,
   Which lives when all is crushed and taken,
The home of dearer than our joy,
   By all save by the soul forsaken
Who strips her clean of doubt and care
Because she breathes her native air,

Yet not for scorn of lovely earth
   And human sweetness born of living,
For these are grown of dearer worth,
   A gift more precious in the giving,
Since through this raiment's hues and lines
The glory of the spirit shines.

Faces of radiant youth, that go
   Like rivers singing to the sea!
You count no careful cost; you know:
   Of that far secret you are free;
And life in you its splendour spending
Sings the stars' song that has no ending.

(July 8, 1915)

AUSTIN DOBSON

Don Quixote

Behind thy pasteboard, on thy battered hack,
Thy lean cheek striped with plaster to and fro,
Thy long spear levelled at the unseen foe,
And doubtful Sancho trudging at thy back,
Thou wert a figure strange enough, good lack!
To make wisacredom, both high and low,
Rub purblind eyes, and (having watched thee go)
Dispatch its Dogberrys upon thy track;
Alas! poor Knight! Alas! poor soul possest!
Yet would to-day when Courtesy grows chill,
And life's fine loyalties are turned to jest,
Some fire of thine might burn within us still!
Ah, would but one might lay his lance in rest,
And charge in earnest . . . were it but a mill!

(1916)

IVOR GURNEY

Going Out at Dawn

Strange to see that usual dark road paving wet
With shallow dim reflecting rain pools, looking
To north, where light all night stayed and dawn braving yet
Capella hung, above dark elms unshaking, no silence
                                        breaking,
And still to dawn night's ugliness owed no debt.

About eleven from the touch of the drear raining,
I had gone in to Shakespeare and my own writing,
Seen the lovely lamplight in golden shining,
And resolved to move no more till dawn made whitening
Between the shutter-chinks, or by the door mat.

Yet here at five, an hour before day was alive . . .
Behold me walking to where great elm trees drip
Melancholy slow streams of rain water, on the too wet
Traveller, to pass them, watching and then return,
Writing Sonata or Quartett with a candle dip.

(Written c.1926, published 1978)

RUDYARD KIPLING

Namely
(Chant Merchant-Maritime of Names)

Such as in Ships of Awesome Size
    Into the seas descend
They roll in suites and toiletries
    And bath-tubs without end.
But me no chromium plumbing thrills
    Or Tudor banquet-hall.
It is her watch and station-bills
    I study more than all.

So, when that first down-Channel night
    Breaks in full gale to day
And Ushant's slavering leagues of white
    Predict a horrid Bay,
Above my early cup of tea,
    Contentedly I think
Of such as have to sail with me.
    Or, peradventure, sink.

Namely: – Port Lifeboat, Twenty-two,
    Bow, Blair, Stroke, Mirrielees.
Falls-Fore and After – [Kinsella], Drew –
    (Both – Heaven be praised – A.B.'s!)
Therewith the first Fifth Engineer,
    And Stewardess Miss White
Detailed to "bring me ladies here,
    And see their belts are right."

So, when that steel four-masted barque,
    Unlit and undermanned,
Looms, leaps, and lunges through the dark
    Entirely out of hand,
And when my chattering tooth-glass tells
    How hard astern we go,

I listen to the urgent bells
    Untroubled for I know

Grant, Hunter, Lindsay, Gordon, Home,
    MacAndrew and McPhee,
On duty in the engine-room,
    Are taking care of me.
While – nine decks up – our helm and screw
    Obedient as his brain –
"The Old Man" subtly brings us through
    And on our course again.

So, when the fog-bank's blinding breath
    Bewilders ear and eye,
And, chillier than the couch of Death
    The unseen berg slips by
On the sports-deck, invisible
    Low-spoken men I hear
Taking the covers off the boats
    And testing davit-gear.

Pratt, Tizard, Banstead, Whitley, Keene,
    Freckleton, Shide, Bellairs –
Deck-hands who rig the weather-screen
    To make a lee for chairs,
And store the toys with which we play
    One hull-board, quoits and rings,
But childish things are put away
    Just now – in case of things.

In the dead hours from one to three
    When even bar-men snore,
I watch the succulent squeejee
    Address the rubber floor.
While, up that damp white avenue
    Of Stewards, suds and smells,
The Carpenter and Mate push through
    To sound our myriad wells.

So, when the whole Atlantic heaves
    Her mountains on our decks,
And the shocked fabric grinds and grieves
    Roars, races, rears and checks,
I do not writhe at every reel,
    Nor wince at every jar.
I know what ship-yard launched her keel
    And whose her engines are.

Which information writ, on brass
    In the companion-way
Is never read by those who pass
    All day and every day
But (without naming any Line)
    So far as I can see
Belfast, Southampton, Clyde and Tyne
    Are good enough for me.

(Written 1935; published 2000)

WILLIAM EMPSON

Letter vi. A Marriage

Rejoice where possible all hares of March
And any daffodils not forced at this date.
I too attempt an epithalamion
Never to be thrust on your unwilling notice
Still less before the public, annotated
    Life's not more strange than this traditional theme.

Terrified by the purity of your dry beauty
Dry tough and fresh as the grass on chalk downs –
The metaphor now seems stale to me only because
It drove me younger to as empty a love –
I have not dared mention to you even the ideal
Version of love sent neatly in typescript
Not altered before publication
And drowned on meeting in my interminable yattering
                                conversation.
    My life's more weak than this traditional theme.

Envisioning however the same beauty in taxiboys
And failing to recognize in one case
What with drink and the infantilism of the Japanese type
The fact that it had not yet attained puberty
I was most rightly (because of another case
Where the jealousy of the driver seemed the chief factor)
 – Not indeed technically, named only in vernacular
                                newspapers,
And who knows who knows –
Deported from that virtuous and aesthetic country;
    Life being as strange as this traditional theme.

I remember only once bathing in the sight of your eyes
Paying some attention to this bloodless series
– One would think to the first – the grey eyes open
Large milky lit fastened steadily on me
Not knowing what to think of what might come next

Supposing I was ever to stop haranguing the tea party;
    There is a social weight on the traditional theme.

It seemed to me impossible to admit that such a signal
(Of which I was certain, which you would now certainly deny)
So dissolving and so noble, had been even recognized,
Still less, having sent them to their owner out of a clownish
                                                    honesty,
To make sensual capital out of writings
Of a sort so much lectured on
As to be practised with decency only for clinical purposes.
    Life is allied to this traditional theme.

Nor am I sure I did not imagine a comparison
 – I was at least hushed and ashamed by those perhaps
                                    misinterpreted eyes –
To the eyes I was to see not long after on my mother,
Thank God not since as yet, cool, liquid, larger than
                                            possible,
Expecting ill-treatment, inquiring, a young girl's,
When after inducing a goodnatured virgin to seduce me
In a morass of mutual misunderstandings, I was kicked out
From a settled job, and hoped I had escaped from you.
    But life was as strange as this traditional theme.

One of these poems at least occurred, long after being
                                            written.
In the next bed to you in a pub in Vienna
I watched the moon shadow of the window upright
Walk clear across neck and face, in perhaps half an hour,
Continually illuminating new beauties,
Placing in you one minute after another everything
I know of admirable in the history of man.
    There is not much more in this traditional theme.

I as in one instant felt during that time
By a trick with time I have known otherwise
Only in the absurd race of an ill-designed chemistry
                                            examination

Where the quarters struck consecutively; but that I won;
Perhaps inversely too in the still photograph
Of shooting a snipe, already behind me, before I knew I had
                                                        tried
 – I am trying to remember triumphs –
    What else but this is the traditional theme?

Maintained one exhausting ecstasy
Interrupted only at moments by a nuisance
A foam of self-consciousness and delight, through which I
                            now know that this occurred.
As the shadow passed to your hair, leaving only truth, I
                                                        spoke.
You woke and understood this at once. A porcine
Expression of complacent pleasure
Rounded with a fine clang my series
Before you turned over and hid the face under the bed
                                                        clothes.
    One could fit this into the traditional theme.

(Written 1935; published 1986)

LOUIS MACNEICE

Departure Platform

Love, my love, it is high time to travel,
　　The brass bell clangs escape
And Summer in a porter's cap will punch our tickets
　　And launch us where the shining lines unravel.

We have been there before though never seen it –
　　The land that was always ours
Whose stones are our bones', whose rivers our blood's
　　　　　　　　　　　　　　　　　kindred;
　　We have never toured that country, only been it.

The distance opens like a mouth to meet us
　　Wantonly tongue to tongue
Consummating our dreams by night, defeating
　　The daily thoughts which day by day defeat us.

Divined but never known – the evasive universal;
　　But fumbling after the scent
Dissolved in the running water of time, we fool our fancy
　　To catch intact what is always in dispersal.

Upon which quest in company with many
　　We hoard our hopes a year
To blow in a fortnight – a dandelion puffball
　　Telling the past time and the spent penny.

So pack like the others, be sure you look your best for
　　This year's unlikely chance;
Whether it is France or Wales or the Canary Islands
　　The place – who knows – is a person to be well dressed
　　　　　　　　　　　　　　　　　　　　for.

Unlikely; and, were that so, I should be jealous
　　Unless that god of the place
Could fuse his person with mine for your enjoyment –

Which nobody knows or, if they knew, would tell us.

But on the off chance pack – your summer frocks and
                                                    sandals
    And a pair of gloves for towns
And one small bottle of scent – Chanel or Coty –
    And your jazz earrings twisted like Christmas candles.

It leaves at three-fifteen – with lifting pistons –
    The zero hour;
Opposite in corner seats we hope for nearness
    And dearness in what is wrongly called the distance.

(1938)

EDMUND BLUNDEN

A Window in Germany

Still the mild shower grows on; amid the drops
The gray gnats loiter or frisk; but we within
Like their sport less. So from my window here,
This ample casement built in the huge old wall
Which even a nunnery might find thick enough,
Barred with old iron branchwork monster-thorned,
I glance into the idle croft below.
I could not find a more familiar scene,
Known from my childhood, known to all my race –
The flagged path from the kitchen of the farm
Into the towsled orchard, plum and pear;
And under boughs of elder the stone sty;
The dog's dish which today he half forgets;
The nettles cluttering up the heaps of logs,
The raspberry-canes scrambling on leaning pales:
An English casual scene, which tells at once
Of rural mastery, and of rural ease.
Thus from my window here in Germany
The pleasant yard-scape shows. The world beyond
Is Sunday evening, and deserves its peace,
After the dogged action of the week,
The harvest battle fought into the night
With lanterns steady or marching; on whose heel
Tremendous thunder flamed and gunned for hours,
Bursting from Weser's vast black-wooded hills.
Such hills, such forests, even such confluent storm
Were not in my old haunt; but it is much
To find the kinship of this quiet house,
Where gentlest goodness lives and constant cure,
And where, from many a nook, far-sundered ghosts,
To whom my ways mean something, gaze on me.

(1939)

ALUN LEWIS

Raiders' Dawn

Softly the civilized
Centuries fall,
Paper on paper,
Peter on Paul.

And lovers waking
From the night –
Eternity's masters,
Slaves of Time –
Recognize only
The drifting white
Fall of small faces
Into the lime.

Blue necklace left
On a charred chair
Tells that Beauty
Was startled there.

(1941)

EDITH SITWELL

Still Falls the Rain
(The Raids, 1940: Night and Dawn)

Still falls the Rain –
Dark as the world of man, black as our loss –
Blind as the nineteen hundred and forty nails upon the
Cross.

Still falls the Rain
With a sound like the pulse of the heart that is changed to
the hammer beat
In the Potter's Field, and the sound of the impious feet.

On the Tomb:
Still falls the Rain
In the Field of Blood where the small hopes breed and the
human brain
Nurtures its greed, that worm with the brow of Cain.

Still falls the Rain
At the feet of the Starved Man hung upon the Cross,
Christ that each day, each night, nails there, have mercy on
us –
On Dives and on Lazarus:
Under the Rain the sore and the gold are as one.

Still falls the Rain –
Still falls the Blood from the Starved Man's wounded Side:
He bears in His Heart all wounds, – those of the light that
died,
The last faint spark
In the self-murdered heart, the wounds of the sad
uncomprehending dark,
The wounds of the baited bear, –
The blind and weeping bear whom the keepers beat
On his helpless flesh . . . the tears of the hunted hare.

Still falls the Rain –
Then – O Ile leape up to my God: who pulles me doune –
See see where Christ's blood streames in the firmament.
It flows from the Brow we nailed upon the tree
Deep to the dying, to the thirsting heart
That holds the fire of the world, – dark-smirched with pain
As Caesar's laurel crown.
Then sounds the voice of One who like the heart of man
Was once a child who among beasts has lain –
"Still do I love, still shed my innocent light, my Blood, for
thee."

(September 6, 1941)

A. L. ROWSE

Charlestown Harbour
(To Christopher away at the War)

In the little port,
Where the ships come rarely now,
In the silence of the street
A thrush sings – you know how:

Causing the echoes to fall
Like flowers upon the quay,
Reaching over the water
To the deserted street and me,

Standing and looking down
Upon the little Dutch ship,
Her tattered flag at mast
Fluttering by the slip.

While, at the harbour-mouth
The wind-awakened sea
Thunders, besieges the pier,
Comes nostrilling over the quay:

And on the outer beach
With dark and sullen roar,
With regular lapse and beat
Breaks upon the shore.

Here in an inland town,
Three hundred miles away,
I hear the sound and taste
The salt rime on the spray:

See before my eye
Harbour-mouth and quay,
Hear the song of a bird,
The remembered surge of the sea.

(1941)

H[ILDA]. D[OOLITTLE].

Ancient Wisdom Speaks to the Mountains

I
Where you are,
your cloak is blue as the robes
the priests of Tibet wear:

where you are,
you stare and stare at a mountain
and a picture of a mountain in the water:

and when the river is half frozen over,
still you stand
snow on your sleeve and hood:

still you stand waiting,
not forgetting;
where were we now

if you had not said over and over,
as you watched the snow
slide down the runnels

and become, below on the slopes,
blossom of apple, quince and the wild-pear,
repeatedly, this prayer:

remember these (you said)
who when the earth-quake shook their city,
when angry blast and fire

broke open their frail door,
did not forget
beauty.

II
O – what a picture of a mountain!
in our desolation,
four times, four seasons

marched up from the valley,
each with its retinue and panoply,
each climbed the mountain slowly:

though the mountain changed its colour
as the seasons came and went,
she did not alter.

III
Her cloak is very old
yet blue as the blue-poppy,
blue as the flax in flower:

and not an hour passed
in our torment
but she thought of us:

she did not change,
the mountain changed from gold to violet,
as the sun rose and set:

she knew our fear,
and yet she did not falter
nor cast herself in anguish by the river:

but she stood,
the sun on her hair
or the snow on her blue hood:

winter and summer,
summer and winter
. . . again . . . again . . .

never forgetting

but remembering
our peculiar desolation:

I will stand here, she said to the mountain,
that even you must start awake, aware
that beauty can endure:

her cloak is very, very old
and blue . . .

(1943)

KEITH DOUGLAS

The Regimental Trumpeter Sounding in the Desert

O how often Arcturus
have you and your companions
heard the laughter and the distant shout
of the long tube a man sets to his mouth
crying that war is sweet, and the men you
see sleep after fighting will fight in the day before us?

Since with manual skill
men dressed to kill in purple
with how many strange tongues
cried the trumpet that cried once
for the death of Hector from Troy steeple
that cried when a hundred hopes fell.

To-night we heard it
who for weeks have only listened
to the howls of inhuman voices.
But as the apprehensive ear rejoiced,
breathing the notes in, the sky glistened
with a flight of bullets. We must be up early.

To-morrow to forget the cry and the crier
as we forgot the conversation
of our friends killed last month, last week
and near, crouching, the air shriek,
the crescendo, expectancy to elation
violently arriving. The trumpet is a liar.

(1943)

ALAN PRYCE-JONES

Twenty-Four Hours' Leave

Other mornings have leaked like cracked glass;
This holds, entire and still.
Calm on the confident freshets of the place
Ripples below our hill
Like light; and on the moving waterface
Unbroken time is wheel.

This holds, entire and still.
I had forgotten how on ruin and grief
Ragged the days fall.
I had forgotten that, and how though brief
When rage is on us all
A whole hour can be safe.

Calm on the confident freshets of the place,
The living calm we knew,
Breathes like a summer through the dear, dear house;
The calm that folded you
Once, when we loved before this anger was
Which makes us two.

Ripples below our hill
Run brightening the wet and silver hay.
We are all summer, and shall
Blaze for the sun, blaze and grow old to-day,
Consume the magical
Reprieve and drop like the warm light and die,

Like light, and on the moving waterface.
Oh, in what bond
Grief draws the springing rivers to distress;
Small in the sky beyond
The inland gulls cry out for loneliness
And faces turned to land.

Unbroken time is wheel.
To-day the long seas sigh within our calm
Faint as a seashell.
The silver haycock and the honeycomb
And the great sun as well
Drop into place. This morning is our home.

(December 25, 1943)

WALTER DE LA MARE

The Winnowing Dream

I saw a Seraph, brighter than the East,
    Who held a rushing fan,
Wherewith, from best to worst from first to least,
    He fanned the thoughts of Man.

Like simple birds that tumble in the air,
    Thin ashes in the sky,
This scattered draff streamed up, unresting there,
    Blown through tempestuously.

Only upon the floor a little grain
    Of Truth lay, strange to see;
The which that Seraph gathered up for gain,
    Man's saving grace to be.

He turned away, mighty in weariness:
    And I in doubt drew near
To scan the little left poor man to bless
    'Gainst his last night of fear.

My heart fell in me, sickened and forlorn;
    Scarce aught of me and mine –
A few poor things of love not yet outworn,
    Sorrow had made divine;

Here, an old childish faith in rueful state,
    There, lost simplicity;
Nothing of much account, rare, subtle, great,
    Nor valued even by me.

(1950)

EDRICA HUWS

The Bonfire

Through the mist and in the entrancing dank
Fullness of the November night a crowd
Stumbled with torch-flash and laugh towards the bank
Where the fire was laid
Above the inscrutable river. Neighbours to to
And fro children calling, stick cracking and loud
Bark of a dog suddenly stopped as through
The straw a small flame played;

Licking about among the old copy books,
Shavings, broken records, gum boots and board,
Breeding with wonderful vigour, shooting out forks,
Shock troops to tackle the hard
Soaked logs which held their line like sweating police
Making a cordon. And all the people stare,
Feasting on destruction, glad that the lease
Of twelve months fret and care

Has fallen in. By proxy purged their eye
Lights with absent innocence, their flesh
Is burnished and their form against the sky
Gilded and jewelled as
An Ikon; so a borrowed sanctity
Seems for a moment theirs until a crash
Flings showers of sparks among the company
Which breaks up where it has

Space to, stepping sideways from the whorls
Of smoke and skirting the bank to miss
The drop into the river. A brand that falls
Is snatched up by a boy
And hurled out over the water, there to meet
Its own reflection with a strangled hiss.
While the roaring logs throw out their heat
A troubled owl gives cry

Hooting among the trees on the other side
Of the river, blinded in his own
Territory, forced in his own hour to make a wide
Detour round the keen
Burning smell that hangs in the damp air
All night and far across the fields is blown.
Even at noon next day ash smoulders where
The bonfire has been.

(1950)

W. H. AUDEN

The Chimeras

Absence of heart – as in public buildings,
Absence of mind – as in public speeches,
Absence of worth – as in goods intended for the public,

Are telltale signs that a chimera has just dined
On someone else; of him, poor foolish fellow,
Not a scrap is left, not even his name.

Indescribable – being neither this nor that,
Uncountable – being any number,
Unreal – being anything but what they are,

And ugly customers for someone to encounter,
It is our fault entirely if we do;
They cannot touch us; it is we who will touch them.

Curious from wantonness – to see what they are like,
Cruel from fear – to put a stop to them,
Incredulous from conceit – to prove they cannot be,

We stroke or kick or measure and are lost:
The stronger we are the sooner all is over;
It is our strength with which they gobble us up.

If someone, being chaste, brave, humble,
Get by them safely, he is still in danger,
With pity remembering what once they were,

Of turning back to help them. Don't.
What they were once was what they would not be,
Not liking what they are not is what now they are.

No one can help them; walk on, keep on walking,
And do no let your goodness self-deceive you:
It is good that they are but not that they are thus.

(1951)

LAWRENCE DURRELL

Sarajevo

Bosnia. November. And the mountain roads
Earthbound but matching perfectly these long
And passionate self-communings counter-march,
Balanced on scarps of trap, ramble or blunder
Over traverses of cloud: and here they move,
Mule-teams like insects harnessed by a bell
Upon the leaf-edge of a winter sky,

And down at last into this lap of stone
Between four cataracts of rock: a town
Peopled by sleepy eagles, whispering only
Of the sunburnt herdsman's hopeless ploy
A sterile earth quickened by shards of rock
Where nothing grows, not even in his sleep,

Where minarets have twisted up like sugar
And a river, curdled with blond ice, drives on
Tinkling among the mule-teams and the mountaineers,
Under the bridges and the wooden trellises
Which tame the air and promise us a peace
Harmless with nightingales. None are singing now.

No history much? Perhaps. Only this ominous
Dark beauty flowering under veils,
Trapped in the spectrum of a dying style:
A village like an instinct left to rust,
Composed around the echo of a pistol-shot.

(1951)

D. J. ENRIGHT

The Laughing Hyena,
by Hokusai

For him, it seems, everything was molten. Court-ladies flow
in gentle streams,
Or, gathering lotus, strain sideways from their curving boat,
A donkey prances, or a kite dances in the sky, or soars like
sacrificial smoke.
All is flux: waters fall and leap, and bridges leap and fall.
Even his tortoise undulates, and his Spring Hat is lively as a
pool of fish.
All he ever saw was sea: a sea of marble splinters –
Long bright fingers claw across his pages, fjords and islands
and shattered trees –

And the Laughing Hyena, cavalier of evil, as volcanic as the
rest:
Elegant in a flowered gown, a face like a bomb-burst,
Featured with fangs and built about a rigid laugh,
Ever moving, like a pond's surface where a corpse has sunk.

Between the raised talons of the right hand rests an object –
At rest, like a pale island in a savage sea – a child's head,
Immobile, authentic, torn and bloody –
The point of repose in the picture : the point of movement in
us.

Terrible enough, this demon. Yet it is present and perfect,
Firm as its horns, curling among its thick and handsome
hair.
I find it an honest visitant, even consoling, after all
Those sententious phantoms, choked with rage and
uncertainty,
Who grimace from contemporary pages. It, at least,
Knows exactly why it laughs.

(1951)

ALAN ROSS

Parks at Tunbridge Wells

Parks takes ten off two successive balls from Wright,
    A cut to the rhododendrons and a hook for six.
    And memory begins suddenly to play its tricks:
I see his father batting, as, if here, he might.

Now Tunbridge Wells, 1951; the hair far lighter,
    The body boyish, flesh strung across thin bone,
    And the arms sinewy as the wrists are thrown
At the spinning ball, the stance much straighter.

Now it is June full of heaped petals,
    The day steamy, tropical; and rain glistens
On the pavilion, shining over corrugated metal.
    The close lush greenness seems to listen.

Then it was Eastbourne, 1935; a date
    Phrased like a vintage, sea-fret on the windscreen.
And Parks, rubicund and squat, busily sedate,
    Pushing Verity square, moving his score to nineteen.

Only a summery image, a snapshot salvaged
    From a seaside of certainty – domed piers
    And speed-boats, a yacht seen through tears
For some lost disappointment, the green hedged.

Cubicle of Then, so neatly parcelled and tied
    By ribbons of war – but now through a chance
    Resemblance re-opened; a son's stance
At the wicket opens the closed years wide.

And it is no good resisting the interior
    Assessment, the fusion of memory and hope
That comes flooding to impose on inferior
    Attainment – yesterday, to-day, twisted like a rope.

Parks drives Wright under dripping green trees,
    The images compare and a father waves away
Applause, pale sea like a rug over the knees,
    Covering him, the son coffining his day

With charmed strokes. And, abstractedly watching,
    Drowning I struggle to shake off the Past,
Whose arms clasp like a mother, and focus the catching
    Despair of our time, summer at half-mast.

The silent inquisitors subside. The crowd,
    Curiously unreal in this regency spa, clap,
A confectionery line under bushes heavily bowed
    In the damp. Then Parks pierces Wright's leg trap.

And we come through, back to the present.
    Sussex 300 for 2. Moss roses on the hill.
A dry taste in the mouth, but the moment
    Sufficient, being what we are, ourselves still.

(1951)

MURIEL SPARK

Chrysalis

We found it on a bunch of grapes and put it
In cotton wool, in a matchbox partly open,
In a room in London in wintertime, and in
A safe place, and then forgot it.

Early in the cold spring we said "See this!
Where on earth did the butterfly come from?"
It looked so unnatural whisking about the curtain :
Then we remembered the chrysalis.
There was the broken shell with what was once
The head askew ; and what was once the worm
Was away out of the window, out of the warm,
Out of the scene of the small violence.

Not strange, that the pretty creature formalized
The virtue of its dark unconscious wait
For pincers of light to come and pick it out.
But it was a bad business, our being surprised.

(1951)

DYLAN THOMAS

Over Sir John's Hill

Over Sir John's hill,
The hawk on fire hangs still;
In a hoisted cloud, at drop of dusk, he pulls to his claws
And gallows, up the rays of his eyes the small birds of the bay
And the shrill child's play
Wars
Of the sparrows and such who swansing, dusk, in wrangling
hedges.

And blithely they squawk
To fiery tyburn over the wrestle of elms until
The flash the noosed hawk
Crashes, and slowly the fishing holy stalking heron
In the river Towy below bows his tilted headstone.

Flash, and the plumes crack,
And a black cap of jack-
Daws Sir John's just hill dons, and again the gulled birds
hare
To the hawk on fire, the halter height, over Towy's fins,
In a whack of wind.
There
Where the elegiac fisherbird stabs and paddles
In the pebbly dab-filled
Shallow and sedge, and, "dilly dilly," calls the loft hawk,
"Come and be killed,"
I open the leaves of the water at a passage
Of psalms and shadows among the pincered sandcrabs
prancing

And hear, in a shell,
Death clear as a buoy's bell:
All praise of the hawk on fire in hawk eyed dusk be sung,
When his viperish fuse hangs looped with flames under the
brand
Wing, and blest shall

Young
Green chickens of the bay and bushes cluck, "dilly dilly,
Come let us die."
We grieve as the blithe birds, never again, leave shingle and
                                                    elm,
The heron and I,
I young Aesop fabling to the near night by the dingle
Of eels, saint heron hyming in the distant

Crystal harbour vale
Where the sea cobbles sail,
And wharves of water where the walls dance and the white
                                            cranes stilt.
It is the heron and I, under judging Sir John's elmed
Hill, tell-tale the knelled
Guilt
Of the led-astray birds whom God, for their breast of whistles,
Have mercy on,
God in his whirlwind silence save, who marks the sparrows
                                                    hail,
For their souls' song.
Now the heron grieves in the weeded verge. Through windows
Of dusk and water I see the tilting whispering

Heron, mirrored, go,
As the snapt feathers snow,
Fishing in the tear of the Towy.   Only a hoot owl
Hollows, a grassblade blown in cupped hands, in the looted
                                                    elms
And no green cocks or hens
Shout
Now on Sir John's hill. The heron, ankling the scaly
Lowlands of the waves,
Makes all the music; and I who hear the tune of the slow,
Wear-willow river, grave,
Before the lunge of the night, the notes on this time-shaken
Stone for the sake of the souls of the slain birds sailing.

(1951)

CHARLES CAUSLEY

General Recall

I saw my captain sail into the bay
 In a glass ship along the reefs of night.
On the white deck her slaughtered pennants lay
 Furled by the scarlet fingers of the fight.
Gagged were the guns that all the dazzled day
 Shouted their speeches at the stammering light.

I saw the sun array his troops of light
 Above the uneasy bastion of the bay,
And all the dour defenders of the night
 Desert my ship, as innocent she lay,
Launching their weapons on the tide, to fight
 For captains, comrades, on a different day.

All though the golden battles of the day
 I heard the bugler blast the alarm of light,
And in the guilty mirror of the bay
 I saw the silver shilling of the night.
On her bold bed the unvirtuous ocean lay
 To lure my hero from the long sea-fight.

Over the green arena of the fight
 I saw the sun advance the device of day,
And all the leaping lancers of the light
 Course their tall horses on the turning bay.
I saw the naked Nubians of the night
 Run from the morning, where she rifled lay.

On the dark deck my sleeping captain lay
 Wrapped in the raving banners of the fight,
Until the sulky linkmen of the day
 Fired with their lamps the secret map of light,
Hurling its wealthy ashes on the bay
 To fee the sentries for the captured night.

Captain, O comrades, when the guns of night
  Feed with black fire the harbour-mouth, and lay
A screen of stars to shield me from the fight
  Or blind my eyes to bandage me from day,
Set me aboard your springing ship of light !
  Set your sail seaward from the punctual bay !

By the wheel lying all the dying night
  I saw my hero strike his flag, and lay
His prize before the levies of the light.

(1952)

ANNE RIDLER

Choosing a Name

My little son, I have cast you out
To hang heels upward, wailing over a world
With walls too wide.

My faith till now, and now my love:
No walls too wide to hold that, and no depth
Too great for all you hide.

I love, not knowing what I love:
I give, though ignorant for whom,
The history and power of a name.

I conjure with it, like a novice
Summoning unknown spirits: answering me
You take the word, and tame it.

Even as the gift of life
You take the strange old name you did not choose
And make it new.

You and the name exchange a power.

Its history is changed, becoming yours,
And yours by this: who calls this, calls you.

Strong vessel of peace, and plenty promised,
Into whose unsounded depths I pour
This alien power:

Frail vessel, launched with a shawl for sail,
Whose guiding spirit keeps the needle-quivering
Poise between trust and terror,

And stares amazed to find himself alive –
This is the means by which you say *I am*;
Not to be lost till all is lost,

When at the sight of God you say *I am nothing*,
And find, forgetting name and speech at last,
A home not mine, dear outcast.

(1952)

SIEGFRIED SASSOON

Another Spring

Aged self, disposed to lose his hold on life,
Looks down, at winter's ending, and perceives
Continuance in some crinkled primrose leaves.

A noise of nesting rooks in tangled trees.
Stillness – inbreathed, expectant.   Shadows that bring
Cloud-castled thoughts from downland distances.
Eyes, ears are old. But not the sense of spring.

Look, listen, live, some inward watcher warns.
Absorb this moment's meaning: and be wise
With hearts whom the first primrose purifies.

(1953)

ROBERT GRAVES

With Her Lips Only

This honest wife challenged at dusk
At the garden gate, under a moon perhaps,
With scent of honeysuckle, dares to deny
Love to an urgent lover: with her lips only,
Not with her heart. It was no assignation;
Taken aback, what could she say else?
For the children's sake, the lie was venial –
"For the children's sake," she argues with her conscience.

Yet a mortal lie must follow before dawn:
Challenged as usual in her own bed
She protests love to an urgent husband,
Not with her heart but with her lips only;
"For the children's sake," she argues with her conscience –
"For the children's sake," growing cold towards them.

(1953)

JOHN BETJEMAN

Norfolk

How did the devil come? When first attack?
    These Norfolk lanes recall lost innocence,
The years fall off and find me walking back
    Dragging a stick along the wooden fence
Down this same path, where, forty years ago,
My father strolled behind me, calm and slow.

I used to fill my hand with sorrel seeds
    And shower him with them from the tops of stiles,
I used to butt my head into his tweeds
    To make him hurry down those languorous miles
Of ash and alder-shaded lanes, till here
Our moorings and the masthead would appear.

Then there was supper lit by lantern light
    And in the cabin I could lie secure
And hear against the polished sides at night
    The lap lap lapping of the weedy Bure,
Dear whispering and watery Norfolk sound
Which told of all the moonlit reeds around.

How did the devil come? When first attack?
    The church is just the same, though now I know
Fowler of Louth restored it. Time, bring back
    The rapturous ignorance of long ago,
The peace, before the dreadful daylight starts
Of unkept promises and broken hearts.

(1953)

V[ITA]. SACKVILLE-WEST

June 2nd, 1953

Madam, how strange to be your Majesty.
How strange to wake in an ordinary bed
And, half awake, to think " Now who am I ?"
As we all think to ourselves when with the dawn
The birds first rouse us with the rising sun
And we recall the little facts of our lives,
The engagements we have that day, the photographs
Framed on the table, the books, the telephone,
And piece the bits of our life together, the worries, the
obligations,
Eventually making, as the cloud of sleep
Disperses, a quick report renewed of our daily self
And of who we are and of what we have to do.

Am I Elizabeth or Lilibet?
Are the Great Officers of State preparing?
Are Charles and Anne asleep in the nursery?

(June 5, 1953)

THEODORE ROETHKE

Elegy for Jane
(My student, thrown by a horse)

I remember the neckcurls, limp and damp as tendrils;
And her quick look, a sidelong pickerel smile;
And how, once startled into talk, the light syllables leaped for
her,
And she balanced in the delight of her thought,
A wren, happy, tail into the wind,
Her song trembling the twigs and small branches.
The shade sang with her;
The leaves, their whispers turned to kissing;
And the mould sang in the bleached valleys under the rose.
Oh, when she was sad, she cast herself down into such a
pure depth,
Even a father could not find her:
Scraping her cheek against a straw;
Stirring the clearest water.

My sparrow, you are not here,
Waiting like a fern, making a spiney shadow.
The sides of wet stones cannot console me,
Nor the moss, wound with the last light.
If only I could nudge you from this sleep,
My maimed darling, my skittery pigeon.
Over this damp grave I speak words of my love:
I, with no rights in this matter,
Neither father nor lover.

(1954)

ROBERT FROST

The Bad Island – Easter
(Perhaps so called because it may have risen once)

That primitive head
So ambitiously vast
Yet so rude in its art
Is as easily read
For the woes of the past
As a clinical chart.
For one thing alone
The success of the lip
So scornfully curled
Has that tonnage of stone
Been brought in a ship
Half way round the world.

They were days on that stone.
They gave it the wedge
Till it flaked from the ledge.
Then they gave it a face.
Then with tackle unknown
They stood it in place
On a cliff for a throne.
They gave it a face
Of what was it? Scorn
Of themselves as a race
For having been born?
And then having first
Been cajoled and coerced
Into being be-ruled?
By what stratagem
Was their cynical throng
So cozened and fooled
And jollied along?
Were they told they were free
And persuaded to see
Something in it for them?

Well they flourished and waxed
By executive guile,
By fraud and by force,
Or so for a while;
Until overtaxed
In nerve and resource
They started to wane,
They emptied the aisle
Except for a few
That can but be described
As a vile residue,
And a garrulous too.
They were punished and bribed;
All was in vain.
Nothing would do.
Some mistake had been made
No book can explain,
Some change in the law
That nobody saw
Except as a gain.
But one thing is sure
Whatever kultur
They were made to parade,
What heights of altrur –
ian thought to attain,
Not a trace of it's left
But the gospel of sharing,
And that has decayed
Into a belief
In being a thief
And persisting in theft
With cynical daring.

(1954)

WILLIAM CARLOS WILLIAMS

The Ivy Crown

THE WHOLE PROCESS is a lie,
          unless,

                         crowned by excess,

it breaks forcefully,
          one way or another,

                         from its confinement –

or find a deeper well.
          Anthony and Cleopatra

                         were right;

they have shown
          the way.   I love you

                         or I do not live

at all.

DAFFODIL TIME
          is past. This is

                         summer, summer!

the heart says,
          and not even the full of it.

                         No doubts

are permitted –
          though they will come

                         and may

before our time
          overwhelm us.

                         We are only mortal

but being mortal
          can defy our fate.

                         We may

by an outside chance
          even win! We do not

                         look to see

jonquils and violets
          come again

                         but there are,

still,

47

the roses!

ROMANCE HAS no part in it.
          The business of love is
                    cruelty which,
by our will,
          we transform
                    to live together.
It has its seasons,
          for and against,
                    whatever the heart
fumbles in the dark
          to assert
                    toward the end of May.

JUST AS THE nature of briars
          is to tear flesh.
                    I have proceeded
through them.
          Keep
                    the briars out,
they say.
          You cannot live
                    And keep free of
the briars.

CHILDREN PICK flowers.
          Let them.
                    Though having them
in hand they have
          no further use for them
                    but leave them crumpled
at the curb's edge.

AT OUR AGE the imagination
          across the sorry facts
                    lifts us
to make roses
          stand before the thorns.

                         Sure

love is cruel
          and selfish

                         and totally obtuse –
at least, blinded by the light,
          young love is.

                         But we are older,
I to love
          and you to be loved,
                         we have,
no matter how,
          by our wills survived
                         to keep
the jewelled prize
          always at our finger tips.
We will it so
          and so it is
                         past all accident.

(1954)

WALLACE STEVENS

Presence of an External Master of Knowledge

Under the shape of his sail, Ulysses,
Symbol of the seeker, crossing by night
The giant sea, read his own mind.
He said, "As I know, I am and have
The right to be." He guided his boat
Beneath the middle stars and said:

"Here I feel the human loneliness
And that, in space and solitude,
Which knowledge is: the world and fate,
The right within me and about me,
Joined in a triumphant vigor,
Like a direction on which I depend . . .

A longer, deeper breath sustains
This eloquence of right, since knowing
And being are one – the right to know
Is equal to the right to be.
The great Omnium descends on me,
Like an absolute out of this eloquence."

The sharp sail of Ulysses seemed,
In the breathings of that soliloquy,
Alive with an enigma's flittering,
And bodying, and being there,
As he moved, straightly, on and on
Through clumped stars dangling all the way.

(1954)

ROY FULLER

Jag and Hangover

I have spent some days of late
Exalted, ambitious, free,
In a stupor of poetry,
And now I open my eyes
To find without much surprise
All incurably second-rate.

The muse's visitations
Fatigue and inflame the sense,
Are precisely as intense
For McGonagalls as for Donnes:
The word appears and stuns
The power to see true relations.

When we desire to say
"Red" and our pen puts down
"Cardinal" all the crown
Of our head becomes alive,
And we imagine five
Or six continents under our sway.

Our ordinary features
Harden to some gold mask;
Like the princess' task
Assumed by dwarfs, the long
History before the song
Can be lived by the singing creatures

Is over, and the earth
Has images for matter.
But soon realities spatter
Both lines and world with dead
Areas where the head
Perceives unsowable dearth.

And so our subject resumes
The massive poverty
From which, improbably,
Tribunes deduce the elate
Harmonious future state
Of rich individual blooms.

(1954)

JOHN BERRYMAN

from "Dream Songs"

I
Huffy Henry hid the day,
unappeasable Henry sulkt.
I see his point – a trying to put things over.
It was the thought that they thought
they could *do* it made Henry wicked & away.
But he should have come out and talkt.

All the world like a woolen lover
once did seem on Henry's side.
Then came a departure.
Thereafter nothing fell out as it might or ought.
I don't see how Henry, pried
open for all the world to see, survived.

What he has now to say is a long
wonder the world can bear and be.
Once in a sycamore I was glad
all at the top, and I sang.
Hard on the land wears the strong sea
and empty grows every bed.

II
– I don't operate often. When I do,
persons take note.
Nurses stare, amazed. They pale.
The patient is brought back to life, or so.
The reason I don't do this more (I quote)
is: I have a living to fail –

because of my wife & son – to keep from earning.
– Mr Bones, I sees that.
They for these operations thanks you, what ?
not pays you. – Right.
You have seldom been so understanding.

Now there is further a difficulty with the light :
I am obliged to perform in complete darkness
operations of great delicacy
on my self.
– Mr Bones, you terrifies me.
No wonder they don't pay you. Will you die ?
My
    friend, I succeeded. Later.

III
Seedy Henry rose up shy in de world
& shaved & swung his barbells, duded Henry up,
and P.A.'d poor thousands of persons on topics of grand
moment to Henry, ah to those less & none.
Wif a book of his in either hand
he is stript down to move on.

Henry is tired of the winter,
& haircuts, & a squeamish comfy / ruin-prone proud
    national mind, / & spring (in the city so called).
Henry likes fall.
He would be prepared to live in a world of fall
for ever, impenitent Henry.
But the snows and summers grieve and dream:

these fierce & airy occupations, and love,
raved away so many of Henry's years
it is a wonder that, with in each hand
one of his own mad books & all,
ancient fires for eyes, his head full
& his heart full, he's making ready to move on.

IV
The Last Dream Song

My daughter's heavier. Light leaves are flying.
Everywhere in enormous numbers turkeys will be dying
& other birds, all their wings.
They never greatly flew. Did they wish to?
I should know. Off away somewhere once I knew
such things.

Or good Ralph Hodgson back then did, or does.
The man is dead whom Eliot praised. My praise
follows & flows too late.
Fall is grievy – brisk. Tears behind the eyes
almost fall. Fall comes to us as a prize
to rouse us toward our fate.

My house is made of wood and it's made well,
unlike us. My house is older than Henry.
That's fairly old.
If there were a middle ground between things & the sun
or if the sky resembled more the sea
I wouldn't have to scold
                                    my heavy daughter.

(1954–66)

NORMAN MACCAIG

The Gifts

You read the old Irish poet and complain
I do not offer you impossible things –
Gloves of bee's fur, cap of the wren's wings,
Goblets so clear light falls on them like a stain.
I make you the harder offer of all I can,
The good and ill that make of me this man.

I need no fancy to mark you as beautiful,
If you are beautiful. All I know is what
Darkens and brightens the sad waste of my thought
Is what makes me your wild, truth-telling fool
Who will not spoil your power by adding one
Vainglorious image to all we've said and done.

Flowers need no fantasy, stones need no dream;
And you are flower, and stone. And I compel
Myself to be no more than possible,
Offering nothing that might one day seem
A measure of your failure to be true
To the greedy vanity that disfigures you.

A cloak of the finest silk in Scotland – what
Has that to do with troubled nights and days
Of anguished happiness? I had no praise
Even of your kindness, that was not bought
At such a price this bankrupt self is all
I have to give. And is that possible?

(1956)

C[ECIL]. DAY LEWIS

View From an Upper Window
(For Kenneth and Jane Clark)

From where I am sitting, my windowframe
Offers a slate roof, four chimneypots,
One aerial, half of a leafless tree,
And sky the colour of dejection. I could
Move my chair; but, London being
What it is, all would look much the same
Except that I'd have the whole of that tree.
Well, window, what am I meant to do
With the prospect you force me to dwell upon – this tame
And far from original aperçu?

I might take the picture for what it can say
Of immediate relevance – its planes and tones,
Though uninspiring, significant because
Like history they happened to happen that way.
Aerial, chimneypots, tree, sky, roof
Outline a general truth about towns
And living together. It should be enough,
In a fluctuating universe, to see they are there
And, short of an atom bomb, likely to stay.
But who wants truth in such everyday wear ?

Shall I, then, amplify the picture? track
The roof to its quarry, the tree to its roots,
The smoke just dawdling from that chimneystack
To the carboniferous age? Shall I lift those slates
And disclose a man dying, a woman agape
With love? Shall I protract my old tree heavenwards,
Or set these aerial antennae to grope
For music inaudible, unborn yet? But why,
If one's chasing the paradigm right forward and back,
Stop at embryo, roots or sky?

Perhaps I should think about the need for frames.
At least they can lend us a certain ability
For seeing a fragment as a kind of whole
Without spilling over into imbecility.
Each of them, though limited its choice, reclaims
Some terra firma from the chaos. Who knows? –
Each of us may be set here, simply to compose
From a few grains of universe a finite view,
By One who occasionally needs such frames
To look at his boundless creation through.

(1957)

PATRICK KAVANAGH

Song at Fifty

It came as a pleasant surprise
To find experience
Where I had feared that I
Had no such currency,
Had idled to a void
Without a wife or child,
I had been looking at
Fields, gates, lakes, all that
Was part and parcel of
The wild breast of love.
In other fellows' wives
I lived a many lives
And here another cries:
My husband I despise
And truth is my true
Husband is you.

So I take my cloak of gold
And stride across the world
A knight of chivalry
Seeking some devilry
The winter trees rise up
And wave me on, a clap
Of falling rock declares
Enthusiasm; flares
Announce a reception committee
For me entering a city.

And all this for an unthrifty
Man turned of fifty;
An undisciplined person
Through futile excitements arsing
Finds in his spendthrift purse
A bank book writ in verse

And borrowers of purity
Offering substantial security
To him who just strayed
Through a lifetime without a trade,
Him, him the ne'er –
Do-well a millionaire.

(1958)

R. S. THOMAS

The Country Clergy

I see them working in old rectories
By the sun's light, by candle-light,
Venerable men, their black cloth
A little dusty, a little green
With holy mildew. And yet their skulls,
Ripening over so many prayers,
Toppled into the same grave
With oafs and yokels. They left no books,
Memorial to their lonely thought
In grey parishes; rather they wrote
On men's hearts and in the minds
Of young children sublime words
Too soon forgotten. God in his time
Or out of time will correct this.

(1958)

HOWARD NEMEROV

Burning the Leaves

This was the first day that the leaves
Came down in hordes, in hosts, a great wealth
Gambled away over the green lawn
Belonging to the house, old fry and spawn
Of the rich year converted into filth
In the beds by the wall, the gutters under the eaves.
We thought of all the generations gone
Like that, flyers, migrants, fugitives.

We come like croupiers with rakes,
To a bamboo clatter drag these winnings in,
Our windfall, firstfruits, tithes, and early dead
Fallen on our holdings from overhead,
And taxable to trees against our sin.
Money to burn! We play for higher stakes
Than the mere leaves, and, burdened with treasure, tread
The orbit of the tree that heaven shakes.

The wrath of God we gather up to-day,
But not for long. In the beginning night
We light our hoarded leaves, the flames arise,
The smell of smoke takes memory by surprise,
And we become as children in our sight.
That is, I think, the object of this play,
Though the children dance about our sacrifice
Unthinking, their shadows lengthened and cast away.

(1959)

MARIANNE MOORE

Saint Jerome and His Lion

Leonardo da Vinci's
    Saint Jerome and his lion
        in that hermitage
  of walls half gone,
        share sanctuary of a sage –
joint frame for impassioned ingenious
        Jerome versed in language
and for a lion like the one on the skin of which
  Hercules' club made no impression.

    The beast, received as a guest,
        although some monks fled ó
  with its paw dressed
        that a desert thorn had made red –
stayed as guard of the monastery ass . . .
        which vanished, having fed
its guard, Jerome assumed. The guest then, like an ass,
  was made carry wood and did not resist,

    but before long, recognized
        the ass and consigned
  its terrorized
        thieves' whole camel train to chagrinned
Saint Jerome. The vindicated beast and
        saint somehow became twinned ;
and now, since they behaved and also looked alike,
  their lionship seems officialized.

    Pacific yet passionate –
        for if not both, how
  could he be great ?
        Jerome – reduced by what he'd been through –
with tapering waist no matter what he ate,
  left us the Vulgate. That in *Leo*,
the Nile's rise grew food that checked famine, made
  lions's-mouth-fountains appropriate,

    if not universally,
        at least not obscure.
    Here, though hardly a summary, astronomy –
        or pale paint – makes the golden pair
In Leonardo da Vinci's sketch seem
        sun-dyed. Blaze on, picture,
saint, beast ; and Lion Haile Selassie, with household
    lions as symbol of sovereignty.

                                                            (1959)

TED HUGHES

View of a Pig

The pig lay on a barrow dead.
It weighed, they said, as much as three men.
Its eyes closed, pink white eyelashes.
Its trotters stuck straight out.

Such weight and thick pink bulk
Set in death seemed not just dead.
It was less than lifeless, further off.
It was like a sack of wheat.

I thumped it without feeling remorse.
One feels guilty insulting the dead,
Walking on graves. But this pig
Did not seem able to accuse.

It was too dead. Just so much
A poundage of lard and pork.
Its last dignity had entirely gone.
It was not a figure of fun.

Too dead now to pity.
To remember its life, din, stronghold
Of earthly pleasure as it had been,
Seemed a false effort and off the point.

Too deadly factual. Its weight
Oppressed me – how could it be moved?
And the trouble of cutting it up!
The gash in its throat was shocking, but not pathetic.

Once I ran at a fair in the noise
To catch a greased piglet
That was faster and nimbler than a cat,
Its squeal was the rending of metal.

Pigs must have hot blood, they feel like ovens.
Their bite is worse than a horse's –
They chop a half-moon clean out.
They eat cinders, dead cats.

Distinctions and admirations such
As this one was long finished with.
I stared at it a long time. They were going to scald it,
Scald it and scrub it like a doorstep.

(1959)

RANDALL JARRELL

The Woman at the Washington Zoo

The saris go by me from the embassies.
Cloth from the moon. Cloth from another planet.
They look back at the leopard like the leopard.

And I – this print of mine, that has kept its color
Alive through so many cleanings; this dull null
Navy I wear to work, and wear from work, and so
To my bed, so to my grave, with no
Complaints, no comments: neither from my chief,
The Deputy Chief Assistant, nor his chief –
Only I complain; this serviceable
Body that no sunlight dyes, no hand suffuses
But, dome-shadowed, withering among columns,
Wavy beneath fountains – small, far-off, shining
In the eyes of animals, these being trapped
As I am trapped but not, themselves, the trap,
Ageing, but without knowledge of their age,
Kept safe here, knowing not of death, for death
– Oh, bars of my own body, open, open!

The world goes by my cage and never sees me.
And there come not to me, as come to these,
The wild beasts, sparrows pecking the llamas' grain,
Pigeons settling on the bears' bread, buzzards
Tearing the meat the flies have clouded . . .
                                        Vulture,
When you come for the white rat that the foxes left,
Take off the red helmet of your head, the black
Wings that have shadowed me, and step to me as man,
The wild brother at whose feet the white wolves fawn,
To whose hand of power the great lioness
Stalks, purring . . .
                    You know what I was,
You see what I am: change me, change me!

(1959)

STEVIE SMITH

Pretty

Why is the word pretty so underrated?
In November the leaf is pretty when it falls
The stream grows deep in the woods after rain
And in the pretty pool the pike stalks.

He stalks his prey, and this is pretty too,
The prey escapes with an underwater flash
But not for long, the great fish has him now
The pike is as fish who always has his prey,

And this is pretty. The water rat is pretty
His paws are not webbed, he cannot shut his nostrils
As the otter can and the beaver, he is torn between
The land and water. Not 'torn', he does not mind.

The owl hunts in the evening and it is pretty
The lake water below him rustles with ice
There is frost coming from the ground, in the air mist
All this is pretty, it could not be prettier.

Yes, it could always be prettier, the eye abashes,
It is becoming an eye that cannot see enough,
Out of the wood the eye climbs. This is prettier
A field in the evening, tilting up.

The field tilts to the sky. Though it is late
The sky is lighter than the hill field
All this looks easy but really it is extraordinary
Well, it is extraordinary to be so pretty,

And it is careless, and that is always pretty
This field, this owl, this pike, this pool are careless
As Nature is always careless and indifferent
Who sees, who steps means nothing, and this is pretty.

So a person can come along like a thief – pretty! –
Stealing a look, pinching the sound and feel,
Lick the icicle broken from the bank
And still say nothing at all, only cry pretty.

Cry pretty, pretty, pretty and you'll be able
Very soon not even to cry pretty
And so be delivered entirely from humanity,
This is prettiest of all, it is very pretty.

(1959)

ALLEN GINSBERG

Death to Van Gogh's Ear

Poet is Priest
Money has reckoned the soul of America
Congress has broken thru to the precipice of Eternity
and the President has built a War machine which will vomit
and rear up Russia out of Kansas
The American Century betrayed by a mad Senate which no
longer sleeps with its wife
Franco has murdered Lorca the fairy son of Whitman
just as Mayakovsky committed suicide to avoid Russia
just as Hart Crane distinguished Platonist committed suicide
to cave in the wrong America
just as millions of tons of human wheat were burned in
secret caverns under the White House
while India starved and screamed and ate mad dogs full of
rain
and mountains of eggs were reduced to white powder and
burned in the halls of Congress
and no godfearing man will walk there again because of the

stink of the rotten eggs of America
and the Indians of Chiapas continue to gnaw their
vitaminless tortillas
aborigines of Australia perhaps gibber in the eggless
wilderness
and I rarely have an egg for breakfast tho my work requires
infinite eggs to come to birth in Eternity
and eggs should be eaten or given to their mothers
and the grief of the countless chickens of America is
expressed in the screaming of her comedians over the
radio
Now Detroit has built a million automobiles of rubber trees
and phantoms
but I walk, I walk, and the Orient walks with me, and all
Africa walks
and sooner or later North America will walk
for as we have driven the Chinese Angel from our door he
will drive us from the Golden Door of the future
Oriental Exclusion act was it 1911
and we have not cherished pity on Tanganyika
and Einstein while alive was mocked for his heavenly
politics
and the immortal Chaplin has been driven from our shores
with the rose in his teeth
Bertrand Russell driven from New York for getting laid
and a secret conspiracy by Catholic Church in the lavatories
of Congress has denied contraceptives to the unceasing
masses of India
and nobody publishes a word that is not the cowardly robot
ravings of a depraved mentality
and the day of the publication of the true literature of the
American body will be the day of Revolution
the revolution of the sexy lamb
the only bloodless revolution that gives away corn
poor Genet will yet illuminate the harvesters of Ohio
And Marijuana is a benevolent narcotic but J. Edgar Hoover
prefers his deathly scotch
And the heroin of Lao-Tze & the Sixth Patriarch is punished
by the electric chair

but the poor sick junkies have nowhere to lay their heads
fiends in our government have invented a cold-turkey cure
   for addiction as obsolete as the Defense Early Warning
                         Radar System.
I am the defense early warning radar system
I see nothing but bombs
I am not interested in preventing Asia from being Asia
and the governments of Russia and Asia will rise and fall
                but Asia and Russia will not fall
and the government of America also will fall but how can
                     America fall
I doubt if anyone will ever fall anymore except governments
fortunately all the governments will fall
the only ones which won't fall are the good ones
and the good ones don't yet exist
But they have to begin existing they exist in my poems
they exist in the death of the Russian and American
                  governments
they exist in the deaths of Hart Crane & Mayakovsky
Now is the time for prophecy without death as a
                consequence
the universe will ultimately disappear
Hollywood will rot on the windmills of Eternity
Hollywood whose movies stick in the throat of God
Yes Hollywood will get what it deserves
Time
with Pentagon demanding millionfold bankruptcy to raise up
            a carnivorous rainbow at Los Alamos
same time building a domed bombproof storage house for
                souls –
to out-monster the billions of Asia?
History will make this poem prophetic and its awful silliness
            a hideous spiritual music
I have the moan of doves and the feather of ecstasy
Man cannot long endure the hunger of the cannibal abstract
War is abstract
the world will be destroyed
but I will die only for poetry, that will save the world
monument to Sacco & Vanzetti not yet financed to ennoble

                                                    Boston
natives of Kenya tormented by idiot con-men from England
South Africa in the grip of the white fool
Vachel Lindsay Secretary of the Interior
Poe Secretary of Imagination
Pound Secty. Economics
and Kra belongs to Kra, and Pukti to Pukti
cross fertilization of Blok and Artaud
Atomic Fusion will warm the Malthusian heart of the West
Sudan irrigated and beauty cities in Sahara
Van Gogh's Ear on the currency -
no more propaganda for monsters
and poets should stay out of politics or become monsters
I have become monsterous with politics
the Russian poet undoubtedly monsterous in his secret
                                                    notebook

Tibet should be left alone
These are obvious prophecies
America will be destroyed
let the Russian poets struggle with Russia
Whitman warned against this "fabled Damned of nations"
Where was Theodore Roosevelt when he sent our warnings
                                    from his castle in Camden
Where was the House of Representatives when Crane read
                                    aloud from his prophetic books
What was Wall Street scheming when Lindsay announced
                                    the doom of Money
the doom of the gory financial sadistic mouth of gold?
Were they listening to my ravings in the locker rooms of
                                    Bickfords Employment Offices?
Did they bend their ears to the moans of my soul when I
    struggled with market research statistics in the Forum at
                                                    Rome?
No, they were fighting in fiery offices, on carpets of
    heart-failure, screaming and bargaining with Destiny
fighting the Skeleton with sabres, muskets, buck teeth,
        indigestion, bombs of larceny, whoredom, rockets,
                                                    pederasty,
back to the wall to build up their wives and apartments,

lawns, suburbs, fairydoms,
Puerto Ricans crowded for massacre on 114th St. for the sake
of an imitation Chinese-Moderne refrigerator
(circa 1930 that was all the style) elephants of mercy
murdered for the sake of an Elizabethan birdcage
millions of agitated fanatics in the bughouse for the sake of
the screaming soprano of industry
Money-chant of soapers toothpaste apes in television sets
deoderizers on hypnotic chairs
petroleum mongers in Texas – jet plane streaks among the
clouds –
sky writers liars in the face of Divinity fanged butchers of
hats and shoes, all Owners, Owners! Owners! with
obsession on property and vanishing Selfhood!
and their long editorials on the fence of the screaming negro
attacked by ants crawled out of the front page
Machinery of a mass electrical dream! A war-creating Whore
of Babylon bellowing over Capitols and Academies!
Money! Money! Money! shrieking mad celestial money of
illusion! Money made of nothing, starvation, suicide!
Money of failure! Money of death!
Money against Eternity! and eternity's strong mills grind out
vast paper of Illusion!

(1959)

PATRICIA BEER

The Other Mariners

I am the mariner who killed,
Unlike most murderers,
Because I wished to keep good luck
Stowed safely behind bars.
I did not reckon on the death
Of the other mariners.

I who dredged God out of the sea
Extinguished all their prayers.
I found grace in an element
Quite different from theirs
And bought forgiveness with the coin
Of the other mariners.

But why did they resent my soul
A thing that no-one shares?
Were they more worthy of my fate
With its unchosen cares?
How welcome to redemption were
The other mariners!

If the survival of one man
Amongst the death of scores
Is commonplace in time of plague
And everyday in wars
Why was mine singled out with oaths
By the other mariners?

Salvation, being a selfish thing,
Knows neither us nor ours.
I do not blame myself or death,
I blame the saving powers
Who made me see the face of God
Not the other mariners.

(1960)

PETER PORTER

Metamorphosis

This new Daks suit, greeny-brown,
Oyster coloured buttons, single vent, tapered
Trousers, no waistcoat, hairy tweed – my own.
A suit to show responsibility, to show
Return to life – easily got for two pounds down,
Paid off in six months – the first stage in the change.
I am only the image I can force upon the town.

The town will have me: I stalk in glass,
A thin reflection in the windows, best
In Jewellers' velvet backgrounds – I don't pass,
I stop, elect to look at wedding rings –
My figure filled with clothes, my putty mask,
A face fragrant with arrogance, stuffed
With recognition – I am myself at last.

I wait in the pub with my Worthington.
Then you come in – how many days did love have,
How can they be catalogued again?
We talk of how we miss each other – I tell
Some truth – You, cruel stories built of men:
"It wasn't good at first but he's improving."
More talk about his car, his drinks, his friends.

I look to the wild mirror at the bar –
A beautiful girl smiles beside me – she's real
And her regret is real. If only I had a car,
If only – my stately self cringes, renders down ;
As in a werewolf film I'm horrible, far
Below the collar – my fingers crack, my tyrant suit
Chokes me as it hugs me in its fire.

(1960)

ROBERT GARRIOCH

Sisyphus

Bumpity down in the corrie gaed whuddran the pitiless
whun stane.
Sisyphus, pechan and sweitan, disjaskit, forfeuchan and
broun'd-aff,
sat on the heather a hanlawhile, houpin the Boss didnae spy
him,
seein the terms o his contract includit nae mention o tea-
breaks,
syne at the muckle big scunnersom boulder he trauchilit
aince mair.
Och ! hou kenspeckle it was, that he kent ilka spreckle and
blotch on't.
Heavin awa at its wecht, he manhaunnlit the bruitt up the
brae-face,
takkin the easiest gagit he had fand in a fudder o dour years,
haudin awa frae the craigs had affrichtit him sair in his
youth-heid,
feelin his years aa the same, gaein cannily, tenty o slipp'd
discs.
Eftir an hour and a quarter he warslit his wey to the brae's
heid,
heystit his boulder richt up on the tap o the cairn (and it
stude there!)
streikit his length on the chuckie-stanes, houpin the Boss
wadnae spy him,
had a wee leuk at the scenery, feenisht a pie and a cheese-
piece.
Whit was he thinking about, that he jist gied the boulder a
wee shove?
Bumpity doun in the corrie gaed whuddran the pitiless whun
stane,
Sisyphus dodderin eftir it, shair o his cheque at the month's
end.

(1963)

EDWIN MORGAN

Canedolia
(An Off-Concrete Scotch Fantasia)

oa! hoy! awe! ba! mey!
who saw?
rhu saw rum. garve saw smoo. nigg saw tain. lairg saw lagg.
rigg saw cigg. largs saw haggs. tongue saw luss. mull saw
yell. stoer saw strone. drem saw muck. gask saw noss. unst
saw cults. echt saw banff. weem saw wick. trool saw twatt.
how far?
from largo to lunga from joppa to skibo from ratho to shona
from ulva to minto from tinto to tolsta from soutra to marsco
from braco to barra from alva to stobo from fogo to fada from
gigha to gogo from kelso to stroma from hirta to spango.
what is it like there?
och it's freuchie, it's faifley, it's wamphray, it's frandy, it's
sliddery.
what do you do?
we foindle and fungle, we bonkle and meigle and maxpoffle.
we scotstarvit, armit, wormit, and even whifflet. we play at
crossstobs, leuchars, gorbals, and finfan. we scavaig, and
there's aye a bit of tilquhilly. if it's wet, treshnish and mishnish.
what is the best of the country?
blinkbonny! airgold! thundergay!
and the worst?
scrishven, shiskine, scrabster, and snizort.
listen! what's that?
Catacol and wauchope, never heed them.
tell us about last night
well, we had a wee ferintosh and we lay on the quiraing. it
was pure strontian!
but who was there?
petermoidart and craigenkenneth and cambusputtock and
ecclemuchty and corriehulish and balladolly and altnacanny
and clauchanvrechan and stronachlochan and auchenlachar
and tighnacrankie and tilliebruaich and killieharra and
invervannach and achnatudlem and machrishellach and

inchtamurchan and auchterfechan and kinlochculter and
ardnawhallie and invershuggle.
and what was the toast?
schiehallion! schiehallion! schiehallion!

(1964)

MERVYN MORRIS

Literary Evening, Jamaica

In a dusty old crumbling building just fit for rats
And much too large for precious poetry-circles,
The culture fans sat scattered in the first ten rows
Listening for English poetry.

Geoff read Larkin beautifully, Enright too,
And Michael Saunders talked between the poems:
"I don't say they are wonderful," he said,
"And would not say that anybody says
They're great. I offer them
As two fair English poets writing nowadays.
They're anti-gesture, anti-flatulence,
They speak their quiet honesties without pretence."

The longer section of the evening's programme
Was poems by the locals, undergraduates,
Some coarse, some wild, and many violent,
All bloody with the strains of rape and childbirth,
Screaming hot curses anti-slavery,
"Down with the limey bastards! up the blacks!
Chr-rist! Let's tear the painted paper
Off all the blasted cracks! "

The more I heard the more it seemed
A pretty rotten choice to read us Larkin,
Dull-mannered, scared, regressive Phil,
Saying No to everything or Soon, Not Yet.
So many bulging poets must have blushed

And wondered where the hell they'd ever get
With noisy poems, brash, self-conscious, colourful,
And feared that maybe they were born too crude.
Maybe they were; but it was bloody rude
Seeming to ask for things that don't belong out here
Where sun shines hot and love is plentiful.

For to us standing here, a naked nation
Bracing ourselves for blows, what use
Is fearfulness and bland negation?
What now if honesty should choose
To say, in all this world's confusion,
That we are still too young for disillusion?

(1964)

ELIZABETH JENNINGS

Mild Ward of a Mental Clinic

Why are we gathered here?
What good will it do?
Some are silent, some speak,
Often one sheds a tear,
Our friends in common are few;
And each of us is weak.

From class and distance we come
And nobody seems to care
(Is this the only good?)
Disease in the dining-room,
All that we think we share –
Unhappiness, black mood.

But if you stand aside
One moment, you're appalled –
Talk of " I, I, I."
And though our ills collide,
All that we suffer's called
By a different name. Some try

To move across the field
Of sickness and of pain.
They suffer when they do.
And yet if one can yield
Compassion, make it plain,
This place will live and grow.

(1964)

SYLVIA PLATH

An Appearance

The smile of iceboxes annihilates me.
Such blue currents in the veins of my loved one!
I hear her great heart purr.

From her lips ampersands and percent signs
Exit like kisses.
It is Monday in her mind: morals

Launder and present themselves.
What am I to make of these contradictions?
I wear white cuffs, I bow.

Is this love then, this red material
Issuing from the steel needle that flies so blindingly?
It will make little dresses and coats,

It will cover a dynasty.
How her body opens and shuts –
A Swiss watch, jeweled in the hinges!

O heart, such disorganization!
The stars are flashing like terrible numerals.
ABC, her eyelids say.

(1966)

UMBERTO SABA
(Translated by Charles Tomlinson)

The Goat

I talked with a goat,
It was alone in its field, tied on a string.
Sated with grass, soaked
Through with the rain, it was bleating.

That unvarying cry
brothered my sorrow. And I
responded, for a joke at first and then because
sorrow is endless and it has
one voice, one note.
That voice I heard
moaning from a solitary goat.

From a goat, with a semitic face, I heard
poured out in plaint, every other grief,
every other life.

(1966)

MIROSLAV HOLUB
(Translated by Jármila and Ian Milner)

Planet

The module made more like a crash-landing.
And on the planet – only fused rocks
and tinder, no spark of life.

Booming.

But the first guards were murdered.
The bodies ripped by fangs
were buried in vain. In the black daylight
they vanished immediately from the stone graves
and next day attacked the living.

They felt that some sort of principle,
vampire in spirit, was waiting here to use
bodies, brains and thoughts
for ends which like darkness like spin like laughter
were fathomless.
And others were devoured and others
among the gored dead stalked the living.
Until it was no longer clear who
still had the original life in him.

The planet stood like the howling of wolves
petrified in timelessness.

There was no point in pretending to be crabs.
They knew, and it knew through them.
They repaired the module and set out for Earth.
Perhaps still human, perhaps also vampires.

And it's not known whether they ever landed.
And it's not known what did land here.
Maybe there are only
symptoms. And booming.
And the strange activity of dead idiots.

(1969)

IAN HAMILTON

Rose

In the delicately shrouded heart
Of this white rose, a patient eye
The eye of love
Knows who I am and where I've been
Tonight, and what I wish I'd done.

I have been watching this white rose
For hours, imagining
Each tremor of each petal to be like a breath
That silences and soothes.

Look at it, I'd say to you
If you were here: it is a sign
Of what is brief, and lonely
And in love.
But you have gone and so I'll call it wise:
A patient breath, an eye, a rose
That opens up too easily, and dies.

(1972)

CHARLES TOMLINSON

The Rich

I like the rich – the way
they say: 'I'm not made of money':
their favourite pastoral
is to think they're not rich at all –
poorer, perhaps, than you or me,
for they have the imagination of that fall
into the pinched decency
we take for granted. Of course,
they do want to be wanted
by all the skivvies and scrapers
who neither inherited nor rose.
But are they daft or deft,
when they proclaim themselves
men of the left, as if prepared
at the first premonitory flush
of the red dawn
to go rushing into the street
and, share by share,
add to the common conflagration
their scorned advantage ?
They know that it can't happen
in Worthing or Wantage:
with so many safety valves
between themselves and scalding,
all they have to fear
is wives, children, breath and balding.
And at worst
there is always some sunny
Aegean prospect. I like the rich –
they so resemble the rest
of us, except for their money.

(1973)

MICHAEL LONGLEY

Swans Mating

Even now I wish that you had been there
Sitting beside me on the riverbank :
The cob and his hen sailing in rhythm
Until their small heads met and the final
Heraldic moment dissolved in ripples.

This was a marriage and a baptism,
A holding of breath, nearly a drowning,
Wings spread wide for balance where he trod,
Her feathers full of water and her neck
Under the water like a bar of light.

(1973)

W. S. GRAHAM

Johann Joachim Quantz's Fourth Lesson

You are early this morning. What we have to do
Today is think of you as a little creator
After the big creator. I know you find
Great joy in the composers, but now you are
In that position where the joy of the flute
Itself is not enough but wants to blow
The great messages into sound. You must
Be faithful to who you are speaking from and yet
It is all right, you will be speaking too.

You are not really only an interpreter.
What you will do is always something else
And they will hear you simultaneously with
The Art you have been given to read. Please
Sit down, and I haven't asked you to take your coat off.

I think the Spring is really coming at last.
I see the canal boys working. I realize
I have not asked you to play on the pipe today.
You must forgive me. I am not myself today.
Be here on Thursday. When you come, bring
Me five herrings. Watch your fingers. Spring
Is apparent but it is still chilblain weather.

(1974)

ANNE SEXTON

Faustus and I

I went to the opera and God was not there.
I was, at the time, in my apprenticeship.
The voices were as full as goblets; in mid-air
I caught them and threw them back. A form of worship.
In those vacant moments when our Lord sleeps
I have the voices. A cry that is mine for keeps.

I went to the galleries and God was not there,
only Mother Roulin and her baby, an old man infant,
his face lined in black and with a strange stare
in his black, black eyes. They seemed to hunt
me down. At the gallery van Gogh was violent
as the crows in the wheat field began their last ascent.

Three roads led to that death. All of them blind.
The sky had the presence of a thousand blue eyes
and the wheat beat itself. The wheat was not kind.
The crows go up immediately like an old man's lies.
The crimes, my Dutchman, that wait within us all
crawled out of that sea long before the fall.

I went to the bookstore and God was not there.
Doctor Faustus was baby blue with a Knopf dog
on his spine. He was frayed and threadbare
with needing. The arch-deceiver and I had a dialogue.
The Debble and I, the Father of Lies himself,
communed, as it were, from the bookshelf.

I have made a pact and a half in my day
and stolen Godes Boke during a love affair,
the Gideon itself for all devout salesmen who pray.
The Song of Solomon was underlined by some earlier pair.
The rest of the words turned to wood in my hands.
I am not immortal. Faustus and I are the also-ran.

(1975)

JOHN ASHBERY

Daffy Duck in Hollywood

Something strange is creeping across me.
La Celestina has only to warble the first few bars
Of "I Thought about You" or something mellow from
Amadigi di Gaula for everything – a mint-condition can
Of Rumford's Baking Powder, a celluloid earring, Speedy
Gonzales, the latest from Helen Topping Miller's fertile
Escritoire, a sheaf of suggestive pix on greige, deckle-edged
Stock – to come clattering through the rainbow trellis
Where Pistachio Avenue rams the 2300 block of Highland
Fling Terrace. He promised he'd get me out of this one.
That mean old cartoonist, but just look what he's
Done to me now! I scarce dare approach me mug's
                                  attenuated
Reflection in yon hubcap, so jaundiced, so *déconfit*
Are its lineaments – fun, no doubt, for some quack
                                  phrenologist's
Fern-clogged waiting room, but hardly what you'd call
Companionable. But everything is getting choked to the point
                                  of
Silence. Just now a magnetic storm hung in the swatch of
                                  sky
Over the Fudds' garage, reducing it – drastically –
To the aura of a plumbago-blue log cabin on
A Gadsden Purchase commemorative cover. Suddenly all is
Loathing. I don't want to go back inside any more. You meet
Enough vague people on this emerald traffic-island – no,
Not people, comings and goings, more: mutterings,
                                  splatterings,
The bizarrely but effectively equipped infantries of
                                  happy-go-nutty
Vegetal jacqueries, plumed, pointed at the little
White cardboard castle over the mill run. "Up
The lazy river, how happy we could be?"
How will it end? That geranium glow
Over Anaheim's had the riot act read to it by the

Etna-size firecracker that exploded last minute into
A *carte du Tendre* in whose lower right-hand corner
(Hard by the jock-itch sand-trap that skirts
The asparagus patch of algolagnic *nuits blanches*) Amadis
Is cozening the Princesse de Clèves into a midnight
                                        micturation spree
On the Tamigi with the Wallets (Walt, Blossom and little
Skeezix) on a lamé barge " borrowed" from Ollie
Of the Movies' dread mistress of the robes. Wait!
I have an announcement! This wide, tepidly meandering,
Civilized Lethe (one can barely make out the maypoles
And *châlets de nécessité* on its sedgy shore) leads to Tophet,
                                        that
Landfill-haunted, not-so-residential resort from which
Some travellers return! This whole moment is the groin
Of a borborygmic giant who even now
Is rolling over on us in his sleep. Farewell bocages,
Tanneries, water-meadows. The allegory comes unsnarled
Too soon; a shower of pecky acajou harpoons is
About all there is to be noted between tornadoes. I have
Only my intermittent life in your thoughts to live
Which is like thinking in another language. Everything
Depends on whether somebody reminds you of me.
That this is a fabulation, and that those "other times"
Are in fact the silences of the soul, picked out in
Diamonds on stygian velvet, matters less than it should.
We live in one dimension, they in ours. While I
Abroad through all the coasts of dark destruction seek
Deliverance for us all, think in that language: its
Grammar, though tortured, offers pavilions
At each new parting of the ways. Pastel
Ambulances scoop up the quick and hie them to hospitals.
"It's all bits and pieces, spangles, patches, really; nothing
Stands alone. What happened to creative evolution?"
Sighed Aglavaine. Then to her Sélysette: "If his
Achievement is only to end up less boring than the others,
What's keeping us here? Why not leave at once?
I have to stay here while they sit in there,
Laugh, drink, have fine time. In my day

One lay under the tough green leaves,
Pretending not to notice how they bled into
The sky's aqua, the wafted-away no-colour of regions
                                                supposed
Not to concern us. And so we too
Came where the others came: nights of physical endurance,
Or if, by day, our behaviour was anarchically
Correct, at least by New Brutalism standards, all then
Grew taciturn by previous agreement. We were spirited
Away *en bâteau*, under cover of fudge dark.
It's not the incomplete importunes, but the spookiness
Of the finished product. True, to ask less were folly, yet
If he is the result of himself, how much the better
For him we ought to be! And how little, finally,
We take this into account! Is the puckered garance satin
Of a case that once held a brace of duelling pistols our
Only acknowledging of that colour? I like not this,
Methinks, yet this disappointing sequel to ourselves
Has been applauded in London and St. Petersburg.
                                        Somewhere
Ravens pray for us."
                    The storm finished brewing. And thus
She questioned all who came in at the great gate, but none
She found who ever heard of Amadis,
Nor of stern Aureng-Zebe, his first love. Some
There were to whom this mattered not a jot: since all
By definition is completeness (so
In utter darkness they reasoned), why not
Accept it as it pleases to reveal itself? As when
Low skyscrapers from lower-hanging clouds reveal
A turret there, an art-deco escarpment here, and last perhaps
The pattern that may carry the sense, but
Stays hidden in the mysteries of pagination.
Not that we see but how we see it, matters; all's
Alike, the same, and we greet him who announces
The change as we would greet the change itself.
All life is but a figment; conversely, the tiny
Tome that slips from your hand is not perhaps the
Missing link in this invisible picnic whose leverage

Shrouds our sense of it. Therefore bivouac we
On this great, blond highway, unimpeded by
Veiled scruples, worn conundrums. Morning is
Impermanent. Grab sex things, swing up
Over the horizon like a boy
On a fishing expedition. No one really knows
Or cares whether this is the whole of which parts
Were vouchsafed – once – but to be ambling on's
The tradition more than the safekeeping of it. This mulch for
Play keeps them interested and busy while the big,
Vaguer stuff can decide what it wants – what maps, what
Model cities, how much waste space. Life, our
Life anyway, is between. We don't mind
Or notice any more that the sky is green, a parrot
One, but have our earnest where it chances on us,
Disingenuous, intrigued, inviting more,
Always invoking the echo, a summer's day.

(1975)

JUDITH WRIGHT

Architects

All buildings type the skeleton
vertical structures braced and strong
with pelvic floor and shoulderbone
the rooms within like organs strung
on muscle, rib and artery,
with corridors of nerve and vein;
threatened by time and gravity.
Buildings depict the shapes of work.

But when the architect must make
the shapes of Parliament and Crown,
of wisdom, art or government,
gallery, temple, library,

he takes the curve, the arch, the dome,
and chooses marble's clarity
to flesh the hard-pressed membrane out.
Skull's swell of thought and memory
houses time past and time to come.

Your head lay heavy on my arm,
so massive, though so delicate,
that love could scarcely bear the weight.

On great Ur-slabs of concrete terraces
or rust-red bones of girder and cross-member
they sit, eating their sandwiches
at noon. They look at home there
among the stylised trunks of metal forests,
the unfinished work.
Maybe the half-built is our proper habitat
manhandling raw material
in basic contact, manipulation, direction
of various substances. Simple . . .

Later, the place changes.
Dressed in plastic wallboards, fitted
with doors and windows, connected
by cables, wires and pipes to the feed-in world
it becomes part of a circuit.

Coming in later to consult officials,
sign papers, buy, sell, argue over contracts,
they observe the fake marble, the carpets
covering those bare encounters of concrete and steel,
the corridors scurrying with unfamiliar errands –
wondering. Wondering about building.
How whatever we construct gets complicated,
gets out of order and beyond control.

(1976)

YEHUDA AMICHAI
(Translated by the author and Ted Hughes)

Like the Inner Wall of a House

I found myself
Suddenly, and too early in life
Like the inner wall of a house
Which has become an outside wall after wars and
                                         devastations.

I almost forget
How it is to be inside. No pain any more,
No love. Near and far
Are both at the same distance from me
And equal.

I never imagined, what happens to colours.
Their fate is man's fate : light blue still slumbers
In the memory of dark blue and night. Paleness
Sighs out of a purple dream. A wind brings smells
From far off
And itself has no smell.
And the leaves of the Huzzar die
Long before their white flower
Which never knows
About the greenness in spring and dark love.

I lift my eyes to the mountains. Now I understand
What it means to lift eyes, what a heavy load
It is. But those hard longings,
That pain-never-again-to-be-inside!

(1976)

ZBIGNIEW HERBERT
(Translated by John Carpenter and Bogdana Carpenter)

Remembering My Father

His face severe in clouds above the waters of childhood
so rarely did he hold my warm head in his hands
given to belief not forgiving faults
because he cleared out woods and straightened paths
he carried the lantern high when we entered the night

I thought I would sit at his right hand
and we would separate light from darkness
and judge those of us who live
– it happened otherwise

a junk-dealer carried his throne on a hand-cart
and the statement of his mortgage the map of our kingdom

he was born for a second time slight very fragile
with transparent skin hardly perceptible cartilage
he diminished his body so I might receive it

in an unimportant place there is shadow under a stone

he himself grows in me we eat our defeats
we burst out laughing
when they say how little is needed
to be reconciled.

(1976)

PHILIP LARKIN

Aubade

I work all day, and get half drunk at night.
Waking at four to soundless dark, I stare.
In time the curtain-edges will grow light.
Till then I see what's really always there :
Unresting death, a whole day nearer now,
Making all thought impossible but how
And where and when I shall myself die.
Arid interrogation: yet the dread
Of dying, and being dead,
Flashes afresh to hold and horrify.

The mind blanks at the glare. Not in remorse
– The good not done, the love not given, time
Torn off unused – nor wretchedly because
An only life can take so long to climb
Clear of its wrong beginnings, and may never;
But at the total emptiness for ever,
The sure extinction that we travel to
And shall be lost in always. Not to be here,
Not to be anywhere,
And soon; nothing more terrible, nothing more true.

This is a special way of being afraid
No trick dispels. Religion used to try,
That vast moth-eaten musical brocade
Created to pretend we never die,
And specious stuff that says *No rational being*
Can fear a thing it will not feel, not seeing
That this is what we fear – no sight, no sound,
No touch or taste or smell, nothing to think with,
Nothing to love or link with,
The anaesthetic from which none come round.

And so it stays just on the edge of vision,
A small unfocused blur, a standing chill
That slows each impulse down to indecision.
Most things may never happen: this one will,
And realisation of it rages out
In furnace-fear when we are caught without
People or drink. Courage is no good:
It means not scaring others. Being brave
Lets no one off the grave.
Death is no different whined at than withstood.

Slowly light strengthens, and the room takes shape.
It stands plain as a wardrobe, what we know,
Have always known, know that we can't escape,
Yet can't accept. One side will have to go.
Meanwhile telephones crouch, getting ready to ring
In locked-up offices, and all the uncaring
Intricate rented world begins to rouse.
The sky is white as clay, with no sun.
Work has to be done.
Postmen like doctors go from house to house.

(1977)

GAVIN EWART

Two Semantic Limericks

1. *According to The Shorter Oxford English Dictionary (1933)*
There existed an adult male person who had lived a relatively short time, belonging or pertaining to St. John's *, who desired to commit sodomy with the large web-footed swimming-birds of the genus *Cygnus* or subfamily *Cygninae* of the family *Anatidae*, characterized by a long and gracefully curved neck and a majestic motion when swimming.
So he moved into the presence of the person employed to carry burdens, who declared: "Hold or possess as something at your disposal my female child! The large web-footed swimming birds of the genus *Cygnus* or subfamily *Cygninae* of the family *Anatidae*, characterized by a long and gracefully curved neck and a majestic motion when swimming, are set apart, specially retained for the Head, Fellows and Tutors of the College."

2. *According to Dr Johnson's Dictionary (Edition of 1765)*
There exifted a person, not a woman or a boy, being in the firft part of life, not old, of St John's* who wifhed to — the large water-fowl, that have a long and very straight neck, and are very white, excepting when they are young (their legs and feet being black, as are their bills, which are like that of a goofe, but fomething rounder, and a little hooked at the lower ends, the two fides below their eyes being black and fhining like ebony).
In consequence of this he moved step by step to the one that had charge of the gate, who pronounced: "Poffefs and enjoy my female offspring! The large water-fowl, that have a long and very straight neck, and are very white, excepting when they are young (their legs and feet being black, as are their bills, which are like that of a goofe, but fomething rounder, and a little hooked at the lower ends, the two fides below their eyes being black and fhining like ebony) are kept in ftore, laid up for a future time, for the fake of the gentlemen with Spanish titles."

* A college of Cambridge University   *(1977)*

HUGH MACDIARMID

Ulysses' Bow

Better violen never screeched on a silken cord
Or kittled a cat's tripes wi's finer-en's,
But the lift is yalla as biest milk,
And the eagle roosts wi' the hens,
And the licht o' life is lourd,
And the voices nocht but men's.

My hert-strings werena broken – then why's he gane
And left them when he canna fin' their marrow
 – A clarsach made for his playin',
A warld to mak' a star o'! –
To the feckless fingers o' sunlicht
Or the litchnin's random arrow ?

(1977)

TONY HARRISON

Three Poems from "The School of Eloquence"

Continuous

James Cagney was the one up both our streets.
His was the only art we ever shared.
A gangster film and choc ice were the treats
that showed about as much love as he dared.

He'd be my own age now in '49 !
The hand that glinted with the ring he wore,
his father's, tipped its treasure into mine
just as the organist dropped through the floor.

He's on the platform lowered out of sight
to organ music, this time on looped tape,
into a furnace with a blinding light
where only his father's ring will keep its shape.

I wear it now to Cagneys on my own
and sense my father's hands cupped round my treat –

they feel as though they've been chilled to the bone
from holding my ice cream all through *White Heat*.

Illuminations: I

The two machines on Blackpool's Central Pier,
The Long Drop and *The Haunted House* gave me
my thrills the holiday that post-war year
but my father watched me spend impatiently:

Another tanner's worth, but then no more!

But I sneaked back the moment that you napped.

Fifty weeks of ovens, and six years of war
made you want sleep and ozone, and you snapped:

Bugger the machines! Breathe God's fresh air!

I sulked all week, and wouldn't hold your hand.
I'd never heard you mention God, or swear,
and it took me until now to understand.

I see now all the piled old pence turned green,
enough to hang the murderer all year
and stare at millions of ghosts in the machine –

the penny dropped in time! Wish you were here!

Collect

Though my mother was already two years dead
Dad kept her slippers warming by the gas,
put hot water bottles her side of the bed,
and still went to renew her transport pass.

You couldn't just drop in. You had to phone.
He'd put you off an hour to give him time
to clear away her things and look alone
as though his still raw love were such a crime.

He couldn't risk my blight of disbelief
though sure that very soon he'd hear her key
scrape in the rusted lock and end his grief –
he *knew* she'd just popped out to get the tea.

I believe life ends with death, and that is all.
You haven't both gone shopping; just the same,
in my new black leather phone book there's your name
and the disconnected number I still call.

(1980)

TOM PAULIN

From "The Book of Juniper"

A clear and tearful fluid,
the bittersweet *genièvre*
is held to a wet window
above a college garden.

On the lazy shores
of a tideless sea,
the Phoenician juniper
burns a fragrant incense
in a sandy nest.

And in a Zen garden
all the miniature trees
have the perfect despair
of bound feet.

Exiled in Voronezh
the leavening priest of the Word
receives the Host on his tongue –
frost, stars, a dark berry,
and the sun is buried at midnight.

*

On a bruised coast
I crush a blue bead
between my fingers
tracing the scent, somewhere,
of that warm mnemonic haybox,
burnished fields, a linen picnic,
and a summer dawn
where mushrooms rise among the stubble.
They are white in the dew
and this nordic grape
whets an eager moment

of naked passion and shrill light.
Its meek astringency is distilled
into perfume and medicines,
it matches venison
as the sour gooseberry
cuts the oily mackerel.
Spicy, glaucous,
its branches fan out:
like the wind's shadow
on long grass,
then melt back
and go to ground
where swart choughs
open their red beaks,
stinging the air
with stony voices.

*

Though it might be a simple
decoration
or a chill fragrance
in a snug souterrain,
I must grasp again
how its green
springy resistance
ducks its head down and skirts
the warped polities of other trees
bent in the Atlantic wind.
For no one knows
if nature allowed it
to grow tall
what proud grace
the juniper tree might show
that flared, once, like fire
along the hills.

*

On this coast
it is the only
tree of freedom
to be found,
and I imagine
that a swelling army is marching
from Memory Harbour and Killala
carrying branches
of green juniper.

Consider
the gothic zigzags
and brisk formations
that square to meet
the green tide rising
through Mayo and Antrim,

now dream
of that sweet
equal republic
where the juniper
talks to the oak,
the thistle,
the bandaged elm,
and the jolly jolly chestnut.

(1980)

FLEUR ADCOCK

An Emblem

Someone has nailed a lucky horse-shoe
beside my door while I was out –
or is it a loop of rubber? No;
it's in two sections. They glide about,
silently undulating: two
slugs in a circle, tail to snout.

The ends link up: it's a shiny quoit
of rippling slug-flesh, thick as a snake,
liquorice-black against the white
paint; a pair of wetly-nak-
ed tubes. It doesn't seem quite right
to watch what kind of love they'll make.

But who could resist? I'll compromise
and give them a little time alone
to nuzzle each other, slide and ooze
into conjunction on their own;
surely they're experts, with such bodies,
each a complete erogenous zone –

self-lubricating, swelling smooth
and boneless under grainy skin.
Ten minutes, then, for them to writhe
in privacy, to slither in-
to position, to arrange each lithe
tapered hose-pipe around its twin.

All right, now, slugs, I'm back; time's up.
And what a pretty coupling I find!
They're swinging from the wall by a rope
of glue, spun out of their combined
mucus and anchored at the top.
It lets them dangle, intertwined,

formally perfect, like some emblem:
heraldic serpents coiled in a twist.
But just in case their pose may seem
immodest or exhibitionist
they've dressed themselves in a cloud of foam,
a frothy veil for love-in-a-mist.

(1981)

JAMES FENTON

A Staffordshire Murderer

Every fear is a desire. Every desire is fear.
The cigarettes are burning under the trees
Where the Staffordshire murderers wait for their accomplices
And victims. Every victim is an accomplice.

It takes a lifetime to stroll to the car park
Stopping at the footbridge for reassurance,
Looking down at the stream observing
(With one eye) the mallard's diagonal progress backwards.

You could cut and run, now. It is not too late.
But your fear is like a long-case clock
In the last whirring second before the hour,
The hammer drawn back, the heart ready to chime.

Fear turns the ignition. The van is unlocked.
You may learn now what you ought to know:
That every journey begins with a death,
That the suicide travels alone, that the murderer needs
company.

And the Staffordshire murderers, nervous though they are,
Are masters of the conciliatory smile.
A cigarette? A tablet in a tin?
Would you care for a boiled sweet from the famous poisoner

Of Rugely? These are his own brand.
He has never had any complaints.
He speaks of his victims as a sexual braggart
With a tradesman's emphasis on the word "satisfaction".

You are flattered as never before. He appreciates
So much, the little things – your willingness for instance
To bequeath your body at once to his experiments.
He sees the point of you as no one else does.

Large parts of Staffordshire have been undermined.
The trees are in it up to their necks. Fish
Nest in their branches. In one of the Five Towns
An ornamental pond disappeared overnight

Dragging the ducks down with it, down to the old seams
With a sound as of a gigantic bath running out,
Which is in turn the sound of ducks in distress.
Thus History murders mallards, while we hear nothing

Or what we hear we do not understand.
It is heard as the tramp's rage in the crowded precinct:
"Woe to the bloody city of Lichfield."
It is lost in the enthusiasm of the windows

From which we are offered on the easiest terms
Five times over in colour and once in monochrome
The first reprisals after the drill-sergeant's coup.
How speedily the murder detail make its way

Along the green beach, past the pink breakers,
And binds the whole cabinet to the oil-drums,
Where death is a preoccupied tossing of the head,
Where no decorative cloud lingers at the gun's mouth.

At the Dame's School dust gathers on the highwayman,
On Sankey and Moody, Wesley and Fox,
On the snoring churchwarden, on Palmer the Poisoner
And Palmer's house and Standfield Hall.

The brilliant moss has been chipped from the Red Barn.
They say that Cromwell played ping-pong with the cathedral.
We train roses over the arches. In the Minster Pool
Crayfish live under carved stones. Every spring

The rats pick off the young mallards and
The good weather brings out the murderers
By the Floral Clock, by the footbridge,
The pottery murderers in jackets of Prussian blue.

"Alack, George, where are thy shoes?"
He lifted up his head and espied the three
Steeple-house spires, and they struck at his life.
And he went by his eye over hedge and ditch

And no one laid hands on him, and he went
Thus crying through the streets, where there seemed
To be a channel of blood running through the streets,
And the market-place appeared like a pool of blood.

For this field of corpses was Lichfield
Where a thousand Christian Britons fell
In Diocletian's day, and and "much could I write
Of the sense that I had of the blood –"

That winter Friday. Today it is hot.
The cowparsley is so high that the van cannot be seen
From the road. The bubbles rise in the warm canal.
Below the lock-gates you can hear mallards.

A coot hurries along the tow-path, like a Queen's Messenger.
On the heli-pad, an arrival in blue livery
Sends the water-boatmen off on urgent business.
News of a defeat. Keep calm. The cathedral chimes.

The house by the bridge is the house in your dream.
It stares through new frames, unwonted spectacles,
And the paint, you can tell, has been weeping.
In the yard, five striped oildrums. Flowers in a tyre.

This is where the murderer works. But it is Sunday.
Tomorrow's bank holiday will allow the bricks to set.
You see ? He has thought of everything. He shows you
The snug little cavity he calls "your future home"

And "Do you know," he remarks, "I have been counting my
                                                victims.
Nine hundred and ninety nine, the Number of the Beast!
That makes you . . ." But he sees he has overstepped the mark:

"I'm sorry, but you cannot seriously have thought you were
the first?"

A thousand preachers, a thousand poisoners,
A thousand martyrs, a thousand murderers –
Surely these preachers are poisoners, these martyrs
murderers?
Surely this is all a gigantic mistake?

But there has been no mistake. God and the weather are
glorious.
You have come as an anchorite to kneel at your funeral.
Kneel then and pray. The blade flashes a smile.
This is your new life. This murder is yours.

(1981)

JOHN FULLER

The College Ghost
(For Hugh Sinclair)

At 11.25, after a college beano
Designed to wish a retiring colleague well
(Who with a glass in one hand, a watch in the other
Like the pieces of Alice's mushroom, sat and then rose
To remind with smiling words why we shall miss him),

At that suspended hour of a summer night,
Having made my few farewells, collected my gown,
My black tie carelessly telling the approximate time,
The claret filling my toes, the toes my shoes
And the shoes knowing more or less the way to go,

I left the smoking-room and paced the cloisters
In the wrong direction, almost three sides where one
Would do, to find the passage to take me safely
To the only place where we regularly fall
Utterly unconscious without rebuke or danger

And came at once upon the college ghost
Lolling in a Gothic arch not far from the kitchen.
It had a gross nonchalant air; pretending
That it simply chanced to be there waiting for no one
Particularly, picking its non-existent nails.

Its face was puffy and indistinct, the eyes
Burnt holes, nose gone, the grin healthy
But upside down. It wore a college scarf
And a row of pens in its shroud like a boffin,
Slouched in its window in a May Week pose.

It watched me as I approached and it made its greeting,
Not deferent, not assertive, simply assuming
Its right to expect me to stop, as though our notes

Had crossed and whatever it was had there and then
To be settled and some confusion straightened out.

The night was dark and winy as a cellar,
The only noises the clacking of the flagpole
On St Swithun's tower and the thumping of my heart.
But I wasn't surprised. I felt it was an encounter
Fated at one or another time to occur.

I fingered the keys in my pocket, the inner and outer
Circuits, comforting brass and heavy for turning
The secret doors and great gates of the college,
Fingered them as though they were amulets
To keep at a distance the presence I found before me.

Behind and through it gleamed the broad green square
Of the lawn where all that summer afternoon
In various attitudes of conversation
Undergraduates had sat with early teas
Outlapping the lingering remains of lunch

And the voice of the shapeless shape, if voice it was,
Drifted towards me softly, catching my ear
Exactly like a carefully-placed loudspeaker,
And its words were the words of all who had sat on that
lawn
Through similar afternoons until such darkness fell:

"Though I am not often seen here, at least at times
When troublesome tasks last through daylight or take
You from page to page of assorted memoranda,
Nose down like a broker or a winded traveller
Frantic for the last train in a foreign city,

"Though I am discrepant and uncorroborated
As a reputation; embarrassing as the memory
Of insufficient words at parting; feared
Like a summons for a forgotten misdemeanour;
Still, I do appear, and appear to you now.

"It's precisely at times like this, when you are distracted
By well-being and owl-light from shutting your senses
To what I represent and am ready to communicate
That I eagerly seize my chance to materialize
Like an image on paper in a paddled tray.

"You reckon you can shortly make your escape,
Say more next time. So be it. That is your manner.
But for the moment, stay. I have something to tell you
That has been keeping but will not keep for ever,
Like Clipsham stone or a Pomerol, but not so nice.

"It concerns the conspiracy to keep me partly asleep
With promise of distinct pleasures belonging to
The forms of success towards which you propelled me,
Wise like an elder framing a constitution
Before he retires and dies a powerless legend.

"You gave me much that could not shame the giver
Whatever whoops of joy and sounds of breakage
Greeted your smiles, fond as a distant uncle,
When the package was ripped open, the contents spilled,
The crucial instructions immediately lost.

"But grammar burned bishops and nations fell to the prism.
I negotiated the quantities of blood required
To put into effect the decrees of the Ineffable.
I argued over heads that I knew were soon
To lose all interest in what they commandeered.

"I was present when the planet first took its header
Into the bracing briny of the impermanent.
I dignified the scribbled with the spacing of nuts and
                                                    muttons.
I bowed in Washington, once the place was invented.
Through me the Greeks discovered Australia.

"Theories of diet dispersed tribes, infections
Accompanied stately truths like interpreters.

I took your towers for wit, your lawns for sorrow,
And made the friendships that reduced brown acres
Of imposing mahogany to the space of a handclasp.

"Even when the world in a more appealing tongue
Spoke of the price to be paid for a share of power,
It was to you I referred with a slight shrug
And perhaps a mock self-deprecatory grin
That could not decide if it cared for your approval.

"You gave it. And that was when I became a ghost.
Rioting invisibly in the halls and staircases
Of my consecrated youth, while everything true
And good fell from my fingers or from windows,
Drifting like laughter in the direction of the ivy.

"Now I appear to you because at last
I have rejoined you for ever. Life has made
Its choice. My affairs are finally quite complete
And there is nothing left in the world to alter.
Whatever you teach will make no difference at all."

So saying, it boyishly scissored the stone sill
With a careless stretch of the arms and a hint of flannel
As the bells in the tower tensed to tell three quarters
And the moon behaved as it likes to do at these moments,
Nodding above the treescape like an impresario.

Which way it went I really couldn't say,
But it had gone. And so I slowly continued
My right-angled path through the heart of the college,
Less light of foot, but somewhat enlightened,
Slightly unsure of what I thought I had heard.

Darkness was all around me like a sixth
Sense, or the absolute quiet of certain music
That the hand trembles to play. And it was like
The world pressing on its pockets of resistance.
Like righteous claims of love. Or threats of war.

And indeed, I thought, the ultimate chaos will surely be
A predicate of just this irresponsible architecture
Of convinced laws and prayers that meddled for years
With the best of fateful intentions until the wind changed.
The words were in my head like an egg in a bottle.

Thoughts too late to unthink: I had the feeling
Of being betrayed by something of my choosing,
Something I had connived at, something belonging
To the projection of a long-suspected failing,
Haunted by the forces it exploits.

(1982)

DOUGLAS DUNN

Land Love

We stood here in the coupledom of us.
I showed her this – a pool of leaping trout,
Split-second saints drawn in a rippled nimbus.

We heard the night-boys in the fir trees shout.
Dusk was an insect-hovered still water,
The calling of lost children, stars coming out.

With all the feelings of a widower
Who does not live there now, I dream my place.
I go by the soft paths, alone with her.

Dusk is a listening, a whispered grace
Voiced on a bank, a time that is all ears
For the snapped twig, the strange wind on your face.

She waits at the door of the hemisphere
In her harvest dress, in the remote
Local August that is everywhere and here.

What rustles in the leaves, if it is not
What I asked for, an opening of doors
To a half-heard religious anecdote?

Monogamous swans on the darkened mirrors
Picture the private grace of man and wife
In its white poise, its sleepy portraitures.

Night is its Dog Star, its eyelet of grief
A high, lit echo of the starry sheaves.
A puff of hedge-dust loosens in the leaves.
Such love that lingers on the fields of life!

(1983)

VERNON SCANNELL

In Memoriam

I remember her as if she still
Waited for me in her fireside chair.
The days do not erase, nor memories fill,
The vacancies in mind and household air.

I remember how competent she was,
Unemotional, except her eyes grew wetter
At pictures of royal babies; she wept because
They looked like mortal kids, though she knew better.

She had no children of her own. Some said
I was like her child, but that was not true;
I was the other-ranks in the army she led,
The spuds behind the flowery garden she grew.

She was a good sort, everyone agreed;
They all said how lucky I was with such a wife,
That despite my being such a broken reed
She enjoyed life. And so she did. My life.

(1983)

C. H. SISSON

In the Raj

He was a tight-lipped devil and a rigorous
Company sergeant-major, I recall
Under the sweaty sky of Barrackpore,
Where all was sweat, where clothes were never dry

And Bengal rot started between our toes.
The sun of Asia! So it seemed to us
And the dead rotting by the Ganges shore
Where melons grow huge but taste of nothing

And the poor lie all day upon the streets
While the exquisite Brahmin minces by.
The air-conditioned and American
Left us to treason and the Queen's red-coats.

Quiet and moderate men, you might say,
Shipped out there, packaged, waiting for our turn
And doing nothing with expiring hope
But drive the kites off from our stinking food.

C. S. M. Birt was adept at all this,
Long enough resident to have prepared
His own devices for a happy life
Or, if not happy, one he could control.

It came first like a rumour in the dark,
Then in the sun, that something was amiss:
The C. S. M. glowered and said less
And what the sepoys said I do not know.

I was elsewhere, a thousand miles away,
When an explicit story reached my ears.
C. S. M. Birt had been under arrest,
Then court-martialled. What the swine had done

Was to sell army pistols in the bazaar.
So far, there was only curiosity.
But then the tale came out. One night the guard
Of Indian Other Ranks had turned out

While Birt said he would check the weapon store.
He took the pistols and accused the guard
– Such turpitude behind those foxy eyes
Which seemed dishonest, abject is what they were.

It was some two years later I saw Birt
And at a depot far from Barrackpore.
With three stripes on my arm I stood outside
The sergeants' mess and Birt came slinking past,

Abashed, silent, shorn of his insolence,
Looking at no one and his face was dead,
The first day out of gaol, a cowed man
Waiting a posting where he was not known.

Different was Curly, now inside the mess:
A rough, soft-spoken man, I do not know
What his crime had been when, years before,
He had done time in a military prison,

Running in circles in the blazing sun.
The N.C.O. in charge threw boxing-gloves
And any man they hit must fight with him,
A bruiser with a pair of bruising gloves.

'Never no more,' Curly would say, 'never no more,
They won't get me again, happen what may.'
He drew a long breath and turned aside
Into the racket of the gramophone.

It was a servile life, the only dream
Was white wings over the fucking cliffs of Dover.
Roll on that fucking boat. Get up them stairs.
And some of the fucking officers was shits.

But one especially, as I remember,
A jumped-up quarter-master, regular,
Who wired a hut to spy upon the men.
It was a round-faced corporal who refused

To obey orders while the wires were there
And in a flash was put behind bars
While sympathetic mates did guard outside.
I do not know the end of that story

Except that two days later he was out,
The wires dismantled and the adjutant
Putting the best face on it that he could.
And I remember other men, six or seven

Years out from home, promised a break at last
Then told they could not go, whose passion would
Have torn the camp up and yet nothing happened,
So impotent was rage against that rule.

Ah servitude! We who have been in chains,
Accepting bitterness for every day,
Now walk as free as any men can be
And know that every pleasure ends in death.

(1983)

GEOFFREY HILL

from "The Mystery of the Charity of Charles Péguy"

Nous sommes les derniers. Presque les après-derniers. Aussitôt après nous commence un autre âge, un tout autre monde, le monde de ceux qui ne croient plus à rien, qui s'en font gloire et orgueil.

(Charles Péguy)

1

Crack of a starting-pistol. Jean Jaurès
dies in a wine-puddle. Who or what stares
through the café-window crêped in powder-smoke?
The bill for the new farce reads *Sleepers Awake*.

History commands the stage wielding a toy gun,
rehearsing another scene. It has raged so before,
countless times; and will do, countless times more,
in the guise of supreme clown, dire tragedian.

In Brutus' name martyr and mountebank
ghost Caesar's ghost, his wounds of air and ink
painlessly spouting. Jauréss blood lies stiff
on menu-card, shirt-front and handkerchief.

Did Péguy kill Jaurés? Did he incite
the assassin? Must men stand by what they write
as by their camp-beds or their weaponry
or shell-shocked comrades while they sag and cry?

Would Péguy answer – stubbornly on guard
among the Cahiers, with his army cape
and steely pince-nez and his hermit's beard,
brooding on conscience and embattled hope?

Truth's pedagogue, braving an entrenched class
of fools and scoundrels, children of the world,

his eyes caged and hostile behind glass –
still Péguy said that Hope is a little child.

Violent contrariety of men and days; calm
juddery bombardment of a silent film
showing such things: its canvas slashed with rain
and St Elmo's fire. Victory of the machine!

The brisk celluloid clatters through the gate;
the cortège of the century dances in the street;
and over and over the jolly cartoon
armies of France go reeling towards Verdun.

2
Rage and regret are tireless to explain
stratagems of the out-manoeuvred man,
the charge and counter-charge. You know the drill,
raw veteran, poet with the head of a bull.

Footslogger of genius, skirmisher with grace
and ill-luck, sentinel of the sacrifice,
without vantage of vanity, though mortal-proud,
defend your first position to the last word.

The sun-tanned earth is your centurion
and you its tribune. On the hard-won
high places the old soldiers of old France
crowd like good children wrapped in obedience

and sleep, and ready to be taken home.
Whatever that vision, it is not a child's;
it is what a child's vision can become.
Memory, Imagination, harvesters of those fields,

our gifts are spoils, our virtues epitaphs,
our substance is the grass upon the graves.
'Du calme, mon vieux, du calme.' How studiously
one cultivates the sugars of decay,

patisserie-tinklings of angels ''sieur-'dame,'
the smile of the dead novice in its plush frame,
while greed and disaffection are ingrained
like chalk-dust in the ranklings of the mind.

'Rather the Marne than the *Cahiers*.' True enough,
you took yourself off. Dying, your whole life
fell into place. ''Sieurs-'dames, this is the wall
where he leaned and rested, this is the well

from which he drank.' Péguy, you mock us now.
History takes the measure of your brow
in blank-eyed bronze, brave mediocre work
of *Niclausse*, *sculpteur*, cornered in the park

among the stout dogs and lame patriots
and all those ghosts, far-gazing in mid-stride,
rising from where they fell, still on parade,
covered in glory and the blood of beetroots.

     *

5
among the beetroots, where we are constrained
to leave you sleeping and to step aside
from the fleshed bayonets, the fusillade
of red-rimmed smoke like stubble being burned;

to turn away and contemplate the working
of the radical soul – instinct, intelligence,
memory, call it what you will – waking
into the foreboding of its inheritance,

its landscape and inner domain; images
of earth and grace. Across Artois the rois-mages
march on Bethlehem; sun-showers fall
slantwise over the kalefield, the canal.

Hedgers and ditchers, quarrymen, thick-shod
curés de campagne, each with his load,
shake off those cares and burdens; they become,
in a bleak visionary instant, seraphim

looking towards Chartres, the spired sheaves,
stone-thronged annunciations, winged ogives
uplifted and uplifting from the winter-gleaned
furrows of that criss-cross-trodden ground.

Or say it is Pentecost: the hawthorn-tree,
set with coagulate magnified flowers of may,
blooms in a haze of light; old chalk-pits brim
with seminal verdure from the roots of time.

Landscape is like revelation; it is both
Singular crystal and the remotest thing.
Cloud-shadows of seasons revisit the earth,
odourless myrrh borne by the wandering kings.

Happy are they who, under the gaze of God,
die for the 'terre charnelle', marry her blood
to theirs, and, in strange Christian hope, go down
into the darkness of resurrection,

into sap, ragwort, melancholy thistle,
almondy meadowsweet, the freshet-brook
rising and running through small wilds of oak,
past the elder-tump that is the child's castle.

Inevitable high summer, richly scarred
with furze and grief; winds drumming the fame
of the tin legions lost in haystack and stream!
Here the lost are blest, the scarred most sacred:

odd village workshops grimed and peppercorned
in a dust of dead spiders, paper-crowned
sunflowers with the bleached heads of rag dolls,
brushes in aspic, clay pots, twisted nails;

the clinking anvil and clear sheepbell-sound,
at noon and evening, of the angelus;
coifed girls like geese, labourers cap in hand,
and walled gardens espaliered with angels;

solitary bookish ecstasies, proud tears,
proud tears, for the forlorn hope, the guerdon
of Sedan, 'oh les braves gens!', English Gordon
stepping down sedately into the spears.

Patience hardens to a pittance, courage
unflinchingly declines into sour rage,
the cobweb-banners, the shrill bugle-bands
and the bronze warriors resting on their wounds.

These fatal decencies, they make us lords
over themselves: familial debts and dreads,
keepers of old scores, the kindly ones
telling their beady sous, the child-eyed crones

who guard the votive candles and the faint
invalid's night-light of the sacrament,
a host of lilies and the table laid
for early mass from which you stood aside

to find salvation, your novena cleaving
brusquely against the grain of its own myth,
its truth and justice, to a kind of truth,
a justice hard to justify. 'Having

spoken his mind he'd a mind to be silent.'
But who would credit that, that one talent
dug from the claggy Beauce and returned to it
with love, honour, suchlike bitter fruit?

9

There is an ancient landscape of green branches –
true *tempérament de droite*, you have your wish –
crosshatching twigs and light, goldfinches
among the peppery lilac, the small fish

pencilled into the stream. Ah, such a land
the Ile de France once was. Virelai and horn
wind through the meadows, the dawn-masses sound
fresh triumphs for our Saviour crowned with scorn.

Good governors and captains, by your leave,
you also were sore-wounded but those wars
are ended. Iron men who bell the hours,
marshals of porte-cochère and carriage-drive,

this is indeed perfection, this is the heart
of the mystère. Yet one would not suppose
Péguy's 'defeat', 'affliction', your lost cause.
Old Bourbons view-hallooing for regret

among the cobwebs and the ghostly wine,
you dream of warrior-poets and the Meuse
flowing so sweetly; the androgynous Muse
your priest-confessor, sister-châtelaine.

How the mood swells to greet the gathering storm!
The chestnut trees begin to thresh and cast
huge canisters of blossom at each gust.
Coup de tonnerre! Bismarck is in the room!

Bad memories, seigneurs? Such wraiths appear
on summer evenings when the gnat-swarm spins
a dying moment on the tremulous air.
The curtains billow and the rain begins

its night-long vigil. Sombre heartwoods gleam,
the clocks replenish the small hours' advance

and not a soul has faltered from its trance.
'Je est un autre', that fatal telegram,

floats past you in the darkness, unreceived.
Connoisseurs of obligation, history
Stands, a blank instant, awaiting your reply:
'If we but move a finger France is saved!'

10
Down in the river-garden a grey-gold
dawnlight begins to silhouette the ash.
A rooster wails remotely over the marsh
like Mr Punch mimicking a lost child.

At Villeroy the copybook lines of men
rise up and are erased. Péguy's cropped skull
dribbles its ichor, its poor thimbleful,
a simple lesion of the complex brain.

Woefully battered but not too bloody,
smeared by fraternal root-crops and at one
with the fritillary and the veined stone,
having composed his great work, his small body,

for the last rites of truth, whatever they are,
or the Last Judgement which is much the same,
or Mercy, even, with her tears and fire,
he commends us to nothing, leaves a name

for the burial-detail to gather up
with rank and number, personal effects,
the next-of-kin and a few other facts,
his arm over his face as though in sleep

or to ward off the sun: the body's prayer,
the tribute of his true passion, for Chartres
steadfastly cleaving to the Beauce, for her,
the Virgin of innumerable charities.

'Encore plus douloureux et doux.' Note how
sweetness devours sorrow, renders it again,
turns to affliction each more carnal pain.
Whatever is fulfilled is now the law

where law is grace, that grace won by inches,
inched years. The men of sorrows do their stint,
whose golgothas are the moon's trenches,
the sun's blear flare over the salient.

J'accuse! j'accuse! – making the silver prance
and curvet, and the dust-motes jig to war
across the shaky vistas of old France,
the gilt-edged maps of Strasbourg and the Saar.

Low tragedy, high farce, fight for command,
march, counter-march, and come to the salute
at every hole-and-corner burial-rite
bellowed with hoarse dignity into the wind.

Take that for your example! But still mourn,
being so moved: éloge and elegy
so moving on the scene as if to cry
'in memory of those things these words were born.'

(1983)

CRAIG RAINE

Gauguin

They going upstair
take longtime lookit shedownstair.

They going upstair
so hedownstair go plenty upstair.

He stickyout number2tongue,
becauses he magnetised to she.

Which she hide in shesecrets,
because she magnetised to he.

They making the mirror, shhh,
numberonetongues completely tied.

Shebody making the horse
and the frog, the safe shescissor,

the squat on the sheback, showing
shekipper tenminute longtime,

till he cry like a candle
and heflame blow out.

Handmake Kodak man, come back,
my secrets are sorry with oil.

(1984)

DEREK MAHON

Death and The Sun
(Albert Camus, 1913-60)

Le Soleil ni la mort ne se peuvent regarder fixement
(La Rochefoucauld)

When the car spun from the road and your neck broke
I was hearing rain on the school bicycle shed
Or tracing the squeaky enumerations of chalk;
And later, while you lay in the *mairie*,
I pedalled home from Bab-el-Oued
To my mother silently making the tea,
Bent to my homework in the firelight
Or watched an old film on television –
Gunfights under a blinding desert sun,
Bogartian urgencies in the Ulster night.

How we read you then, admiring the frank composure
Of a stranger bayed by dogs who could not hear
The interior dialogue of flesh and stone,
His life and death a work of art
Conceived in the silence of the heart.
Not that he would ever have said so, no,
He would merely have taken a rush-hour tram
To a hot beach white as a scream,
Stripped to a figure of skin and bone
And struck out, a back-stroke, as far as he could go.

Deprived though we were of his climactic privileges
And raised in a northern land of rain and murk
We too knew the familiar foe, the blaze
Of headlights on a coast road, the cicadas
Chattering like watches in our sodden hedges;
Yet never imagined the plague to come,
So long had it crouched there in the dark –
The *cordon sanitaire*, the stricken home,

Rats on the pavement, rats in the mind,
'St James Infirmary' playing to the plague wind.

'An edifying abundance of funeral parlours',
The dead on holiday, cloth-caps and curlers,
The shoe-shine and the thrice-combed wave
On Sunday morning and Saturday night;
Wee shadows boxing in a smoky cave
Who would one day be brought to light –
The modes of pain and pleasure,
These were the things to treasure
When times changed and your kind broke camp:
Diogenes in the dog-house, you carried a paraffin lamp.

Meanwhile in the night of Europe, the winter of faces,
Sex and opinion, a deft hand removes
The *Just Judges* from their rightful places
And hangs them behind a bar in Amsterdam –
A desert of fog and water, a cloudy dream
Where an antique Indonesian god grimaces
And relativity dawns like a host of doves;
Where the artist who refused suicide
Trades solidarity for solitude,
A night watch, a self-portrait, supper at Emmaus.

The lights are going on in towns that no longer exist.
Night falls on Belfast, on the just and the unjust,
On its Augustinian austerities of sand and stone –
While Sisyphus' descendants, briefly content,
Pause at their factory gates to light a Gitane.
Malraux described these preterite to you
As no longer historically significant;
And certainly they are shrouded in white dust.
All souls leprous, blinded by truth, each ghost
Steams on the shore as if awaiting rescue . . .

One cannot stare for long at death or the sun.
Imagine Plato's Neolithic troglodyte
Released from his dark cinema, released even

From the fire proper, so that he stands at last,
Absurd and anxious, out in the open air
And gazes, shading his eyes, at the world there –
Tangible fact ablaze in a clear light
That casts no shadow, where the vast
Sun gongs its lenity from a brazen heaven;
And beyond that an empty wilderness
Waiting in silence for his upraised voice.

(1985)

PETER READING

Eavesdropped

'Sensitive things them Topical Rain Forests,
regulates all the Global Humility,
    neccitates Nature Conversation,
        otherwise animals Mass Distinction.'

'Gie im a pint quick – diggin is grave wi is
prick e is, this bloke: seen im on Satdy night
    parked in the Quarry, winders steamed-up,
        flattened them oats o mine, randy fuckerrr.'

'Tell you what, old chap, strictly between ourselves,
I have a *leetle* personal whatsaname –
    utterly vital I drink daily,
        huge amounts, otherwise get so damn sad.'

(1986)

MICHAEL HOFMANN

Wheels

Even the piss-artist, rocking back and forth
on the balls of his feet like a musical policeman,
is making an irreversible commitment. . . . He shivers.

(The faith, application and know-how it takes
to do anything, even under controlled circumstances!)
I find in myself this absurd purposefulness;

walking through my house, I lean forward,
I lick my finger to open a door, to turn over a page,
or the page of a calendar, or an advent calendar.

It takes all day to read twenty pages,
and the day goes down in a blaze of television.
One blue day is much like another . . . . The plane lands

with a mew of rubber and a few "less-than" signs.
The ball, remembering who hit it, keeps going.
The choreographed car-chase is ruinously exciting,

but the wheels turn very slowly backwards,
to convince the viewer that, far from wasting time,
he's recreating himself. A Christmas Special!

From the great outdoors, there's the derision
of real cars, the honeyed drone of approachable taxis,
some man's immortal Jag, numbered RAMISH. . . .

How it must cut past the huddle of water-blue Inyacars,
lining the elbow of the road: smashed imperatives,
wheelchair hulls, rhombuses, stalled quartz.

(1986)

ALAN BROWNJOHN

Observation Car

At last they arranged it so you just couldn't see
Out of any train window. You had to focus
On the back seat in front, or the floor, or on
The obligatory food, wheeled up on trolleys
To where they had strapped you in; though a favoured few
Could end up riding at the rear of the train
In the Observation Car, from where the lines receding
Added ever-increasing length to the two sides
Of angle wedging acutely into the past.
How fast that terrain seemed; and interesting,
Though it vanished before you guessed it had ever been:
You saw your bridges after you had crossed them,
You learnt what had been before you saw it coming,
And everyone pointed and said, 'The amazing things
We were missing all that time! If we had known,
We might have stopped the train and got out to enjoy them!'
 – In this assuming they were better off
Than the others sitting boxed in their airline seats
And observing nothing. When, occasionally,
Someone did complain to the guardian who came
Down the gangway cancelling tickets, he would say,
'You are fortunate to have seats, either there or here,
In the midst of such a good metaphor for life.'

(1986)

JOSEPH BRODSKY

May 24th, 1980

I have braved, for want of wild beasts, steel cages,
carved my term and nickname on bunks and rafters,
lived by the sea, flashed aces in an oasis,
dined with the-devil-knows-whom, in tails, on truffles.
From the height of a glacier I beheld half a world, the
                                    earthly
width. Twice have drowned, thrice let knives rake my nitty-
                                    gritty.
Quit the country that bore and nursed me.
Those who forgot me would make a city.
I have waded the steppes that saw yelling Huns in saddles,
worn the clothes nowadays back in fashion in every quarter,
planted rye, tarred the roofs of pigsties and stables,
guzzled everything save dry water.
I've admitted the sentries' third eye into my wet and foul
dreams. Munched the bread of exile; it's stale and warty.
Granted my lungs all sounds except the howl;
switched to a whisper. Now I am forty.
What should I say about life? That it's long and abhors
                                  transparence.
Broken eggs make me grieve; the omelette, though, makes
                                  me vomit.
Yet until brown clay has been crammed down my larynx,
only gratitude will be gushing from it.

(1987)

KATHLEEN JAMIE

Child with Pillar Box and Bin Bags

But it was the shadowed street-side she chose
while Victor Gold the bookies basked
in conquered sunlight, and though
Dalry Road Licensed Grocer gloried and cast
fascinating shadows she chose
the side dark in the shade of tenements;
that corner where Universal Stores' (closed
for modernization) blank hoarding blocked
her view as if that process were illegal;
she chose to photograph her baby here,
the corner with the pillar box.
In his buggy, which she swung to face her.
She took four steps back, but
the baby in his buggy rolled toward the kerb.
She crossed the ground in no time
it was fearful as Niagara;
she ran to put the brake on, and returned
to lift the camera, a cheap one.
The tenements of Caledonian Place neither
watched nor looked away, they are friendly buildings.
The traffic ground, the buildings shook, the baby breathed
and maybe gurgled at his mother as she
smiled to make him smile in his picture;
which she took on the kerb in the shadowed corner;
beside the post-box, under tenements, before the
bin-bags hot in the sun that shone
on them, on dogs, on people on the other side
the other side of the street to that she'd chosen,
if she'd chosen or thought it possible to choose.

(1988)

THOM GUNN

Death's Door

Of course the dead outnumber us
– How their recruiting armies grow!
My mother archaic now as Minos,
She who died forty years ago.

After their processing, the dead
Sit down in groups and watch TV,
In which they must be interested,
For on it they see you and me.

These four, who though they never met
Died in one month, sit side by side
Together in front of the same set
And all without a *TV Guide*.

Arms round each other's shoulders loosely,
Although they can feel nothing, who
When they unlearned their pain so sprucely
Let go of all sensation too.

Thus they watch friend and relative
And life here as they think it is
– In black and white, repetitive
As situation comedies.

With both delight and tears at first
They greet each programme on death's stations,
But in the end lose interest,
Their boredom turning to impatience.

'He misses me? He must be kidding
– This week he's sleeping with a cop.'
'All she reads now is *Little Gidding*.'
'They're getting old. I wish they'd stop.'

The habit of companionship
Lapses – they break themselves of touch:
Edging apart at arm and hip,
Till separated on the couch

They woo amnesia, look away
As if they were not yet elsewhere,
But when snow blurs the picture they,
Turned, give it a belonging stare.

Snow blows out toward them, till their seat
Filling with flakes becomes instead
Snow-bank, snow-landscape, and in that
They find themselves with all the dead,

Where passive light from snow-crust shows them
Both Minos circling and my mother.
Yet none of the recruits now knows them,
Nor do they recognize each other,

They have been so superbly trained
Into the perfect discipline
Of an archaic host, and weaned
From memory briefly barracked in.

(1988)

CHRISTOPHER REID

Amphibiology

Like old men frolicking in sacks
Seals slither on the sea-thrashed rocks.

Why does their melancholy sport
Exert such a strong pull on my heart?

I could stand here for hours on end
Watching them fail to make dry land.

From time to time one gains brief purchase,
Adopting the pose of a Grand Duchess.

In seconds, though, a fist of surf
Rises to swipe the pretender off.

Repetitive slapstick, it has the charm
Of earliest documentary film.

Studded statesmen and wind-up warriors
Turn to salute us across the years . . .

Only, in this case, something far
More ancient seems to hang in the air.

It could be the question, whether to plump
For a great evolutionary jump,

Or stay put in the icy brine.
May the Good Lord send them a hopeful sign!

(1988)

KIT WRIGHT

Short Afternoons

Who would suppose a dryad in a laburnum
Accusing over a privet hedge? Or the woman
Who asks me the way and stares deep in my eyes
As though reading an autocue in them?
But we have entered

The country of short afternoons where every angle
Is filled with intense implication. Brickwork is pertinent,
Sycamore leaves
The wind scrapes widdershins over the pavement
Are freighted with dangerous meaning, a world

At your two-timing feet and its secret truth on the tip
Of your tongue. In the sky
A vapour trail is a pipe-cleaner metamorphosing
Into a papery silver birch limb, changing
Into a spoilage into the lake of darkness,

Sun knowing sudden
Disgrace as it falls from the arms of the tree of heaven.
And then the silver,
Black and too purple
Frieze is under vindictive construction,

Wind in its element again
Of chaos and old night. So faces
That dip after work into pubs on the Holloway Road
Are electrical, tripped
Into such sudden transparency,

Into such lit significance there is reason
To fear and cherish, to huddle and talk excitedly,
Naming each other's names, since faces
Are offered once only, says the wind,
And the singable circumstance is being alive.

(1989)

CAROL ANN DUFFY

In Your Mind

The other country, is it anticipated or half-remembered?
Its language is muffled by the rain which falls all afternoon
one autumn in England, and in your mind
you put aside your work and head for the airport
with a credit card and a warm coat you will leave
on the plane. The past fades like newsprint in the sun.

You know people there. Their faces are photographs
on the wrong side of your eyes. A beautiful boy
in the bar on the harbour serves you a drink – what? –
asks you if men could possibly land on the moon.
A moon like any orange drawn by a child. No.
Never. You watch it peel itself into the sea.

Sleep. The rasp of carpentry wakes you. On the wall,
a painting lost for thirty years renders the room yours.
Of course. You go to your job, right at the old hotel, left,
then left again. You love this job. Apt sounds
mark the passing of the hours. Seagulls. Bells. A flute
practising scales. You swap a coin for a fish on the way
                                                        home.

Then suddenly you are lost but not lost, dawdling
on the blue bridge, watching six swans vanish
under your feet. The certainty of place turns on the lights
all over town, turns up the scent on the air. For a moment
you are there, in the other country, knowing its name.
And then a desk. A newspaper. A window. English rain.

(1990)

KINGSLEY AMIS

Matin
(Or: Homage to Mogadona)

Awake at last, groaning with relief,
In dull daylight, I struggle to remember,
Then promptly to forget, that clouded scene
(Urban always) full of unknown people
Busy at something, talking, hurrying,
Perhaps searching or playing. Not that they
Ignore me, no, they are most interested;
They move closer with rapid hands and eyes
And what must be machines, tall ones, small ones
That dart about like animals, and animals
Like no animals anywhere. And I
Have to get out, or get home, find my book,
Or find my wife. What is this place?
Three jockeys – are they jockeys? – strut forward,
Walls lurch and crinkle, a dark sky shows through;
A headless bulk bobs at me, stirring up
Only sluggish bewilderment, not fear,
Not so much fear.
             Awake at last, I huddle,
Swill water, grope for glasses, slippers; now
Mocktown must fade, but not the small thought
Of being suddenly back
Among the frozen tramcars and thick poppies
With no daylight at the end.

(1990)

GLYN MAXWELL

Sport Story of a Winner

He was a great ambassador for the game.
        He had a simple name.
His name was known in households other than ours.
        But we knew other stars.
We could recall as many finalists
        as many panellists.
But when they said this was his Waterloo,
        we said it was ours too.

His native village claimed him as its own,
        as did his native town,
adopted city and preferred retreat.
        So did our own street.
When his brave back was up against the wall,
        our televisions all
got us shouting and that did the trick.
        Pretty damn quick.

His colours were his secret, and his warm-up
        raindance, and his time up
Flagfell in the Hook District, and his diet
        of herbal ice and his quiet
day-to-day existence and his training,
        and never once explaining
his secret was his secret too and his book
        and what on earth he took

that meant-to-be-magic night in mid-November.
        You must remember:
his game crumbled, he saw something somewhere.
        He pointed over there.
The referees soothed him, had to hold things up.
        The ribbons on the Cup
were all his colour but the Romanoff
        sadly tugged them off.

We saw it coming, didn't we. We knew
        something he didn't know.
It wasn't the first time a lad was shown
        basically bone.
Another one will come, and he'll do better.
        I see him now – he'll set a
never-to-be-beaten time that'll last forever.
        Won't he, Trevor.

(1990)

LES MURRAY

It Allows a Portrait in Line-Scan at Fifteen

He retains a slight "Martian" accent, from the years of single
        phrases.
He no longer hugs to disarm. It is gradually allowing him
        affection.
It does not allow proportion. Distress is absolute, shrieking,
and runs him at frantic speed through crashing doors.
He likes cyborgs. Their taciturn power, with his intonation.
It still runs him around the house, alone in the dark, cooing
        and laughing.
He can read about soils, populations and New Zealand. On
        neutral topics he's illiterate.
Arnie Schwarzenegger is an actor. He isn't a cyborg really,
        is he, Dad?
He lives on forty acres, with animals and trees, and used to
        draw it continually.
He knows the map of Earth's fertile soils, and can draw it
        freehand.
He can only lie in a panicked shout *SorrySorryIdidn'tdoit!*
        warding off conflict with others and himself.

When he ran away constantly it was to the greengrocers to
worship stacked fruit.
His favourite country was the Ukraine: it is nearly all deep
fertile soil.
When asked to smile, he photographs a rictus-smile on his
face.
It long forbade all naturalistic films. They were Adult
movies.
If they (that is, he) *are bad the police will put them in*
hospital.
He sometimes drew the farm amid Chinese or Balinese rice
terraces.
When a runaway, he made uproar in the police station,
playing at three times adult speed.
Only animated films were proper. Who Killed Roger Rabbit
then authorised the rest.
Phrases spoken to him he would take as teaching, and
repeat.
When he worshipped fruit, he screamed as if poisoned when
it was fed to him.
A one-word first conversation: *Blane – Yes! Plane, that's*
right, baby! – Blane.
He has forgotten nothing, and remembers the precise quality
of experiences.
It requires rulings: *Is stealing very playing up, as bad as*
murder?
He counts at a glance, not looking. And he has never been
lost.
When he ate only nuts and dried fruit, words were for dire
emergencies.
He'd begun to talk, then returned to babble. It withdrew
speech for years.
He remembers all the breeds of fowls, and all the counties of
Ireland.
Is that very autistic, to play video games in the day?
He is anger's mirror, and magnifies any near him, raging it
down.
It still won't allow him fresh fruit, or orange juice with bits
in it.

He swam in the midwinter dam at night. It had no rules
about cold.
He was terrified of thunder and finally cried as if in
explanation It – angry!
He grilled an egg he'd broken into bread. Exchanges of
soil-knowledge are called landtalking.
He lives in objectivity. I was sure Bell's palsy would leave
my face only when he said it had begun to.
Don't say word! when he was eight forbade the word
"autistic" in his presence.
Bantering questions about girlfriends cause a terrified look
and blocked ears.
He sometimes centered the farm in a furrowed American
Midwest.
Eye contact, Mum! means he truly wants attention. It
dislikes I contact.
He is equitable and kind, and only ever a little jealous. It
was a relief when that little arrived.
He surfs, bowls, walks for miles. For many years he hasn't
trailed his left arm while running.
I gotta get smart! Looking terrified into the years. *I gotta
get smart!*

(1994)

SEAMUS HEANEY

Mycenae Lookout

Cities of grass. Fort walls. The dumbstruck palace.
I'd come to with the night wind on my face,
Agog, alert again, but far, far less

Focused on victory than I should have been –
Still isolated in an old disdain
Of claques who always needed to be seen

And heard as the true Argives. Mouth athletes,
Quoting the oracle and quoting dates,
Petitioning, accusing, taking votes.

No element that should have carried weight
Out of the grievous distance would translate.
Our war stalled in the pre-articulate.

The little violets' heads bowed on their stems,
The pre-dawn gossamers, all dew and scrim
And star-lace, it was more through them

I felt the beating of the huge time-wound
We lived inside. My soul wept in my hand
When I would touch them, my whole being rained

Down on myself, I saw cities of grass,
Valleys of longing, tombs, a wind-swept brightness,
And far-off, in a hilly, ominous place,

Small crowds of people watching as a man
Jumped a fresh earth-wall and another ran
Amorously, it seemed, to strike him down.

(1994)

ANDREW MOTION

Tortoise

This is a man who served his generals faithfully
and over the years had everything shot away
starting from the feet and working upwards:
feet, legs, chest, arms, neck, head.
In the end he was just a rusting helmet
on the lip of a trench. Then his chin-strap went.

So he became a sort of miraculous stone,
miraculous not just for the fine varnish
which shows every colour right to the depths –
black, topaz, yellow, white, grey, green –
but for the fact it can move. You see?
Four legs and a head and off he goes.

There's only one place to find the future now –
right under his nose – and no question either
where the next meal might be coming from:
jasmine, rose, cactus, marigold, iris, oleander
all snow their flowers round him constantly
and all in their different ways are so delicious.

It explains why there is no reason to hurry.
The breeze blows, the blossoms fall, and the head
shambles in and out as the mouth munches:
Remorseless, tight, crinkled, silent, toothless, pink.
Life is not difficult any more, oh no; life is simple.
It makes you pause, doesn't it. It makes you think.

(1995)

PETER REDGROVE

The Mortier Water-Organ Called Oscar

I
The Mortier Water-Organ, multi-media watershow,
Slides fountain into fountain, where they stand
Jetting inside each other, welding their coiffures

Before two small Georgian mansions made of mist
And sliding water rear to one great salon
Whose collapsing colonnades are tiling-scaled

Like Fishmonger's Hall; it simplifies itself
Into a tide of jellyfish, radiant flounces
Whose tiers are foam-constructed. Now

Shunting-yards of fast bright trains
Speed towards each other and yes
Crash but also splash

Into a highrise museum
Towering with glassy casements
Galleries and halls displaying

Specimens of light from all directions. A giant's
Fourfold spinning mirror-polished mousetrap
Showers as it snaps shut, then dilates

Sustaining barrel-ceilings pelting with a cloudburst
Where rainbow-lightnings play at disco-beat
Of blood-red, sky-blue, gold-snaking jets

Trimmed with black fountain-hedges, silver-sleeved,
Stripping skin off skin over hymen portals
Doors opening on doors which are freshly opening.

II
I sniffed at her neck; I saw
A tall and mobile fountain,
A noble fountain plashing over silver.

In the sheeted tabernacle of rhythms
I touched her back, her lungs
Beating like birds' wings, sturdy
Little lobed birds;

The weather turns
Over and over, apparently
With sublime indifference, only
It brings such dreams and images;
The mighty waves gush forth
And stain our garments.

III
Two skins in bed
Watching each other
Through the one skin
They had made, first
A fine fuzz like a peach patting
Their souls, then
Silky feathers of a moth, dabbing
At that light, then
The roucheness of a toad
Clasping desperately in
Blessed amplexus. What
Infinite eyes as the night
Opens in us!

IV
Oscar, the Mortier Organ, built
In the mad mid-Twenties for a Belgian Dance Hall.

This overture with organ pipes and percussion concludes,
The water-ballet turns into a firework-show,

The skeletons of pipes flute-perforated
Playing their innumerable solos
In shower-cages of searchlights
Or spinning astrolabes water-spouting.

Strange, while I am watching
I forget the music and see only

The unaccompanied visions and the white noise
Of the radically-altering water like

The background hiss of the stars.

V
That is how we met Oscar, who knew
What we did in bed together, and made
A public spectacle of it, thank Goodness,
Under the stars made of rolling quintessence,
At the mercy of perpetual inner fountains.

(1996)

MARK FORD

Plan Nine

The dreadful telephone again: gentle as a kitchen
He'd walk through snow to lay his wreath or convey
Misgivings. The signal fades, freeing me to crawl
Through cold Friday, to forage amid the shadows cast
By a reckless crowd of brittle soap-opera characters.
Our bodies drag, halt mesmerized, lurch forward
With a yelp. "What's the story, morning glory?"
Inquires the super, whose reign of terror
And mind like glue leave less than ever
To be desired. I drink my Rhenish, though it tastes
Of poison, and attack with everything
Until at last the bugle sounds. Briskly, beyond
These streaming drapes, a caustic voice unfolds the case
To a clutch of bright-eyed interns; no mohair, no alcohol,
Lots of plain yoghurt certainly, no foreign languages, no
                                      tête à têtes.

(1996)

BERNARD O'DONOGHUE

Ter Conatus

Sister and brother, nearly sixty years
They'd farmed together, never touching once.
Of late she had been coping with a pain
In her back, realization dawning slowly
That it grew differently from the warm ache
That resulted periodically
From heaving churns on to the milking-stand.

She wondered about the doctor. When,
Finally, she went, it was too late,
Even for chemotherapy. All the same,
She wouldn't have got round to telling him,
Except that one night, watching television,
It got so bad she gasped, and struggled up,
Holding her waist. "D'you want a hand?", he asked,

Taking a step towards her. "I can manage",
She answered, feeling for the stairs.
Three times, like that, he tried to reach her.
But, being so little practised in such gestures,
Three times the hand fell back, and took its place,
Unmoving at his side. After the burial,
He let things take their course. The neighbours watched

In pity the rolled-up bales, standing
Silent in the fields, with the aftergrass
Growing into them, and wondered what he could
Be thinking of: which was that evening when,
Almost breaking with a lifetime of
Taking real things for shadows,
He might have embraced her with a brother's arms.

(1997)

PAUL MULDOON

Third Epistle to Timothy

You made some mistake when you intended to favor me
with some of the new valuable grass seed. . . for what you
gave me. . . proves mere timothy.
(A letter from Benjamin Franklin to Jared Eliot, July 16, 1747)

I

Midnight. June, 1923. Not a stir except for the brough and
brouhaha
surrounding the taper or link
in which a louse
flares up and a shadow, my da's,
clatters against a wall of the six-by-eight-by-six foot room
he sleeps in, eleven years old, a servant-boy at Hardy's of
Carnteel.
There's a boot-polish lid filled with turps
or paraffin oil
under each cast-iron bed-leg, a little barrier
against bed-bugs under each bed-foot.

II

That knocking's the knocking against their stalls of the team
of six black Clydesdales mined in Coalisland
he's only just helped to unhitch from the cumbersome
star of a hay-rake. Decently and in order
he brought each whitewashed nose
to its nosebag of corn, to its galvanised bucket.
One of the six black Clydesdale mares
he helped all day to hitch and unhitch
was showing, on the near hock, what might be a bud of
farcy
picked up, no doubt, while on loan to Wesley Cummins.

III

"Decently and in order," Cummins would proclaim, "let all

Inniskillings

be done." A week ago my da helped him limber up
the team to a mowing-machine as if to a gun-carriage. "For
no Dragoon
can function without his measure of char."
He patted his belly-band. "A measure, that is, against
dysentery."
This was my da's signal to rush
into the deep shade of the hedge to fetch such little tea as
might remain
in the tea-urn. "Man does not live", Cummins would snort,
"only by scraps
of wheaten farls and tea-dregs.
You watch your step or I'll see you're shipped back to
Killeter."

IV

"Kill*eeshill*," my da says, "I'm from Kill*eeshill*." Along the
cast-iron
rainbow of his bed-end
comes a line
of chafers or cheeselips that have scaled the bed-legs
despite the boot-polish lids. Eleven years of age. A servant-
boy
on the point of falling asleep. The reek of paraffin
or the pinewoods reek
of turpentine
good against roundworm in horses. That knocking against
their stalls
of six Clydesdales, each standing at sixteen hands.

V

Building hay even now, even now drawing level with the
team's head-brass,
buoyed up by nothing more than the ballast
of hay – meadow cat's-tail, lucerne, the leaf upon trodden leaf
of white clover and red –
drawing level now with the taper-blooms of a horse chestnut.
Already light in the head.

"Though you speak, young Muldoon . . ." Cummins calls up
                         from trimming the skirt
of the haycock, "Though you speak with the tongue
of an angel, I see you for what you are. . . Malevolent.
Not only a member of the church malignant but a
                         malevolent spirit."

VI

Even now borne aloft by bearing down on lap-cocks and
                         shake-cocks
from under one of which a ruddy face
suddenly twists and turns upwards as if itself carried
on a pitchfork and, meeting its gaze,
he sees himself, a servant-boy still, still ten or eleven,
breathing upon a Clydesdale's near hock and finding a
                         farcy-bud
like a tiny glow in a strut of charcoal.
"I see you," Cummins points at him with the pitchfork, "you
                         little byblow,
I see you casting your spells, your sorceries,
I see you coming as a thief in the night to stab us in the
                         back."

VII

A year since they kidnapped Anketell Moutray from his
                         home at Favour Royal,
dragging him, blindfolded, the length of his own gravel path,
eighty years old, the Orange county grand master. Four A
                         Specials shot on a train
in Clones. The Clogher valley
a blaze of flax-mills and haysheds. Memories of the Land
                         League. Davitt and Biggar.
Breaking the boycott at Lough Mask.
The Land Leaguers beaten
at the second battle of Saintfield. It shall be revealed. . .
A year since they cut out the clapper of a collabor. . . a
                         collabor. . .
A collaborator from Maguiresbridge.

VIII
That knocking's the team's near-distant knocking on wood
while my da breathes upon
the blue-yellow flame on a fetlock, on a deep-feathered
pastern
of one of six black Shires. . . "Because it shall be revealed by
fire,"
Cummins's last pitchfork is laden
with thistles, "as the sparks fly upward
man is born into trouble. For the tongue may yet be cut
from an angel." The line of cheeselips and chafers
along the bed-end. "Just wait till you come back down and I
get a hold
of you, young Muldoon . . . We'll see what spells you'll cast."

IX
For an instant it seems no one else might scale
such a parapet of meadow cat's-tail, lucerne, red and white
clovers,
not even the line of chafers and cheeselips
that overthrow as they undermine
when, light in the head, unsteady on his pegs as Anketell
Moutray,
he squints through a blindfold of clegs
from his grass-capped, thistle-strewn vantage point,
the point where two hay-ropes cross,
where Cummins and his crew have left him, in a straw hat
with a fraying brim,
while they've moved on to mark out their next haycock.

X
That next haycock already summoning itself from windrow
after wind-weary windrow
while yet another brings itself to mind in the acrid stink
of turpentine. There the image of Lizzie,
Hardy's last servant-girl, reaches out from her dais
of salt hay, stretches out an unsunburned arm
half in bestowal, half beseechingly, then turns away to
appeal

to all that spirit-troop
of hay-treaders as far as the eye can see, the coil on coil
of hay from which, in the taper's mild uproar,
they float out across the dark face of the earth, an earth
                                    without form, and void.

(1997)

SIMON ARMITAGE

The Good Ship Melancholia

Bring out the dead, delivered, washed of flesh.
Then in the shipyards of the bays and coves
begin the ark. The bones to build the hull,
the ribs and spines to form the struts and keel.
Uphold the superstructure of a skull.

A crucifix or mawkin for a mast.
A black-out curtain for a flag. For sails
the Turin shroud, unravelled from above,
filled with the moans of passengers and crew.

Put out to sea. Let fly a rook or crow
to bring back news of willow, elder, yew,
a living cockroach in its beak. Not so,

that bird comes back a dove, unhands itself
like one white glove applauding one white glove.

(1997)

IVAN LALIC
(Translated from Serbo-Croat by Francis R. Jones)

Genius Loci

If you rehearse long enough the art of return
To the selfsame place,
                        which finally starts
To remember you, like some stubborn coincidence,

If you return long enough to grow old in the shade
Of the same, more permanent image, don't be surprised
To hear water splash in the chill of a cistern,
To see the flash of an eel, fleshed lightning, or
The wet death of an insect (though you know full well
That in the cistern is dust, crumbling walls,
And a sloughed snakeskin),
                        for wisdom here is older
Than illusion: strange, at times, are the rewards
For loyalty to things less quick to change –
In the cleft of the snake's tongue, time quivers
And slips back into itself;
                        and so you become
Clairvoyant, in one compassionate direction, towards
The gleam of an image which has no memory of you:
Look how the sea shimmers through the thinning panes –

The sole blessing of a place you love.

(1997)

JOHN BURNSIDE

Autobiography

It was late on a winter's evening;
travelling home from work on a crowded train
and stopping from time to time at a quiet station
to wait amidst the nothing that was there
between the darkness and the platform lamps,

and I'll never know quite who it was, when a single
thread of my being stood up and opened the door,
the night air chilling his skin and the smell of water
finding its own dark level in his lungs,
the entire train groaning and throbbing as it drew

away from the empty platform, leaving
only this stain of blood-heat on the snow:
a not-quite-human creature, all regret
and muted terror seeping from his throat
like old smoke, or the heat of eucalyptus.

(1999)

HUGO WILLIAMS

Mirror History

Round about here I become aware of your
existence for the first time, that you might even
be alive, in the sense that I am alive,
walking around having thoughts about everything,
but keeping a pleasant expression on your face.
I wonder why it never struck me before
that you might not be happy all the time.

When I think about lovemaking for instance,
it occurs to me that you might not have been
faking it after all, that perhaps it was me
who was putting on an act for your benefit.
As if you couldn't read me like a book!
How strange to think there were two of us
doing those things and I never realized.

Re-reading what I have written up till now
I am conscious only of what is not being said,
the mirror history running underneath all this
self-pitying nonsense. To hear me talk
you'd think I was the aggrieved party,
whereas we both know it was my own decision
to do nothing that made nothing happen.

Even as we were breaking up for the last time
I was looking at my watch behind your back,
Thinking: what shall we do next? Through my tears
I made out the hands telling me I was late
for something or other, so I cut short my visit
and went dashing off across London on the bike,
telling myself I could always go back if I wanted to.

If only they were waiting for us somewhere,
the nights we didn't use, the things we didn't do,
the bridge we didn't lean on in the moonlight,
watching the barges pass beneath our feet.
Instead, a faint glimmer appears on the horizon,
as if someone were signalling through mist.
A ghost with a yellow shopping bag
waves to a yellow raincoat
at the other end of a street.

(1999)

Acknowledgements

The Editors and TSL Education Ltd. gratefully acknowledge the following:

Macmillan Publishers for Thomas Hardy's "Song of the Soldiers"; Samuel French Publishers for John Drinkwater's "The Ships of Grief"; Oxford University Press for Robert Bridges's "Hell and Hate"; Society of Authors for Laurence Binyon's "The Cause"; H. A. Dobson for Austin Dobson's "Don Quixote"; Carcanet Press for Ivor Gurney's "Going Out at Dawn"; A P Watt for Rudyard Kipling's "Namely"; Curtis Brown for William Empson's "Letter vi. a Marriage"; David Higham and Associates for Louis MacNeice's "Departure Platform"; Peters, Fraser and Dunlop for Edmund Blunden's "A Window in Germany"; Seren Books for Alun Lewis's "Raiders' Dawn"; David Higham and Associates for Edith Sitwell's "Still Falls the Rain"; John Johnson Limited for A. L. Rowse's "Charlestown Harbour"; Normal Holmes Pearson for Hilda Doolittle's "Ancient Wisdom Speaks to the Mountain"; J. C. Hall for Keith Douglas's "The Regimental Trumpeter Sounding in the Desert"; David Pryce-Jones for Alan Pryce-Jones's "Twenty-Four Hours' Leave"; The Society of Authors for Walter de la Mare's "The Winnowing Dream"; Curtis Brown for W. H. Auden's "The Chimeras"; Curtis Brown for Lawrence Durrell's "Sarajevo"; D. J. Enright for "The Laughing Hyena, by Hokusai"; Jane Ross for Alan Ross's "Parks at Tunbridge Wells"; Muriel Spark for "Chrysalis"; David Higham and Associates for Dylan Thomas's "Over Sir John's Hill"; David Higham and Associates for Charles Causley's "General Recall"; Carcanet for Anne Ridler's "Choosing a Name"; George T. Sassoon for Siegfried Sassoon's "Another Spring"; A P Watt for Robert Graves's "With Her Lips Only"; Curtis Brown for John Betjeman's "Norfolk"; Nigel Nicholson for Vita Sackville-West's "June 2nd, 1953"; Peter A. Gilbert for Robert Frost's "The Bad Island, Easter"; Declan Spring for William Carlos Williams's "The Ivy Crown"; John Fuller for Roy Fuller's "Jag and Hangover"; Kate Donoghue for an excerpt from John Berryman's "Dream Songs"; Curtis Brown for Cecil Day Lewis's "View from an Upper Window"; The Estate of R. S. Thomas for "The Country Clerk"; The Ted Hughes Estate for "View of a Pig"; Peter Porter for "Metamorphosis"; New Beacon Books for Mervyn Morris's "Literary Evening in Jamaica"; Edwin Morgan for "Canedolia"; Carcanet for Elizabeth Jennings's "Mild Ward of a Mental Clinic"; Faber and Faber for Sylvia Plath's "An Appearance"; David Young for his translation of Miroslav Holub's "Planet"; Ian Hamilton for "Rose"; Charles Tomlinson for "The Rich"; Michael Longley for "Swans Mating"; John Ashbery for "Daffy Duck in Hollywood"; Shiel Land Associates for Yehuda Amichai's "Like the Inner Wall of a House"; John and Bogdana Carpenter for their translation of Zbigniew Herbert's "Remembering My Father"; Faber and Faber for Philip Larkin's "Aubade"; Margot Ewart and Hutchinson for Gavin Ewart's "Two Semantic Limericks"; Tony Harrison for three poems from "The School of Eloquence"; Tom Paulin for an excerpt from "The Book of Juniper"; Fleur Adcock for "An Emblem"; James Fenton for "A Staffordshire Murderer"; John Fuller for "The College Ghost"; Douglas Dunn for "Land Love"; Vernon Scannell for "In Memoriam"; C. H. Sisson for "In the Raj"; Geoffrey Hill for extracts from "The Mystery of the Charity of Charles Péguy"; Craig Raine for "Gauguin"; Derek Mahon for "Death and the Sun"; Peter Reading for "Eavesdropped"; Michael Hofmann for "Wheels"; Alan Brownjohn for "Observation Car"; Ann Kjellberg for Joseph Brodsky's "May 24th, 1980"; Kathleen Jamie for "Child with Pillar Box and Bin Bags"; Thom Gunn for "Death's Door"; Christopher Reid for "Amphibiology"; Kit Wright for "Short Afternoons"; Glyn Maxwell for "Sport Story of a Winner"; Carol Ann Duffy for "In Your Mind"; Martin Amis for Kingsley Amis's "Matin"; Les Murray for "It Allows a Portrait in Line-Scan at Fifteen"; Seamus Heaney for "Myceanae Lookout"; Andrew Motion for "Tortoise"; Mark Ford for "Plan Nine"; Peter Redgrove for "The Mortier Water-Organ Called Oscar"; Bernard O'Donoghue for "Ter Conatus"; Paul Muldoon for "Third Epistle to Timothy"; Simon Armitage for "The Good Ship Melancholia"; Francis R. Jones for his translation of Ivan Lalic's "Genius Loci"; John Burnside for "Autobiography"; Hugo Williams for "Mirror History".

At the time of going to press every effort has been made to trace the holders of copyright in the case of poets no longer alive. We apologise for any unavoidable omissions.